# REPORTING THE WAR
## THE JOURNALISTIC COVERAGE OF WORLD WAR II

# REPORTING THE WAR

## THE JOURNALISTIC COVERAGE OF WORLD WAR II

FREDERICK S. VOSS

SMITHSONIAN INSTITUTION PRESS FOR THE NATIONAL PORTRAIT GALLERY, WASHINGTON, D.C.

# CONTENTS

An exhibition at the National Portrait Gallery, Washington, D.C., April 22 through September 5, 1994

This exhibition has been made possible in part through a grant from Scripps Howard. In-kind support was made possible by *Life* magazine. Additional assistance was provided by the Smithsonian Institution Special Exhibition Fund, the Smithsonian Women's Committee, and the Smithsonian Research Opportunities Fund.

Library of Congress Cataloging-in-Publication Data
Voss, Frederick.
Reporting the war : the journalistic coverage of world war II / Frederick S. Voss.
p. cm.
Includes bibliographic references and index.
ISBN 1-56098-349-3 (cloth : alk. paper). — ISBN 1-56098-348-5 (pbk : alk. paper).
1. World War, 1939–1945—Journalists. 2. World War , 1939–1945—Journalism, Military, United States. 3. Press—United States—History—20th century. I. Title.
D798.V67 1994
940.54`8173—dc20                    93-36113

British Library Cataloging-in-Publication data available

00 99 98 97 96 95 94  5 4 3 2 1

∞ The paper used in this publication meets the minimum requirements of the American National Standard for Permanence of Paper for Printed Library Materials Z39.48-1984.

For permission to reproduce any of the illustrations, correspond directly with the sources. The Smithsonian Institution Press does not retain reproduction rights for these illustrations individually or maintain a file of addresses for photo sources.

Cover illustration: *Bar at the Hotel Scribe* (detail) by Floyd Davis (1896–1966). Oil on canvas, 48.3 x 73.7 cm (19 x 29 in.), 1944. National Portrait Gallery, Smithsonian Institution, Washington, D.C. Illustrated in full on p. 194.

Front matter illustrations: *(Opposite title page) William Shirer at French surrender at Compeigne, June 1940* by unidentified photographer (see p. 131); *(opposite contents page) Saipan, June 1944* by W. Eugene Smith (see p. 71).

Photography Credits
*Wayne Geist:* 128 (microphone), 151
*Mac's Photography:* 114, 116
*Walter Scott:* 128 (telegram)
*Joseph Szaszfai:* 29
*Rolland White:* cover, 99, 141, 143, 146, 147, 148, 152–53, 154, 156, 157, 160, 161, 167, 180, 194, 199
*Photograph courtesy National Archives:* 110

Printed in Canada

# FOREWORD

ALAN FERN
DIRECTOR, NATIONAL PORTRAIT GALLERY

Fifty years ago, the events of World War II were the daily concern of everyone in the United States of America. It is hard to recapture the flavor of that time for generations with a different view of patriotism and national purpose, and a far more negative view of warfare as a national undertaking than was prevalent in the 1940s. Back then, every family was touched in fundamental ways by the global conflict. Virtually everyone had a close relative at war or working in a war plant. Everyone had to participate in the rationing of food, petroleum fuel, clothing, and commodities to allow the redirection of agricultural, refining, and manufacturing industries to the supply of the military effort. No new civilian cars were built between 1942 and 1946, changing the habits of millions of consumers who had traded in their automobiles every other year or so, even during the Great Depression; now gas was strictly rationed, tires were unavailable, and even parts were hard to find. Unexpectedly, there was little resistance to these hardships—although they were strictures that would never have been tolerated in normal times.

The American attitude toward the Second World War was unlike anything this nation has experienced before or since. Years of preparation had molded public opinion, so there was a widespread belief that the forcible German expansion into the countries neighboring its borders and the Japanese invasion of China—beginning with the takeover of Manchuria in 1931—were evil schemes plotted by villainous warlords. Stories of atrocities, and caricatures of the perpetrators, had been disseminated in newspapers, magazines, and even bubblegum trading cards; movie plots reflected these new attitudes at first subtly, later more blatantly; and newsreels, radio commentaries, and other communications media provided vivid reinforcement for what was fast becoming a national consensus.

Nevertheless, there was initially strong opposition to American involvement in the effort to halt Germany's drive for hegemony over Europe and Japan's pursuit of the same goal in the Asian Pacific. The most powerful group of opponents—some of them in Congress—believed that the United States had no business interfering in conflicts between sovereign states far from our shores. Their view was that no matter how violent, illegal, or immoral Germany's and Japan's territorial aggressions might be, the United States was insulated from the conflicts by vast oceans and by a different set of national and economic interests and ought to stay out of conflicts in remote places. Others felt that they could not wholeheartedly support an American war effort, because they were treated as second-class citizens and felt little inclination to make sacrifices for a nation that dealt with them so shabbily. A third, and far smaller, group was actually in sympathy with the Axis cause.

In the face of all this, President Franklin Delano Roosevelt, who did see a need for American intervention, had to move cautiously, and sometimes secretively at first, in committing the United States to a more active involvement in opposing Japan and Germany. However, with the Japanese bombardment of navy and army installations at Pearl Harbor, Hawaii, on December 7, 1941, the national mood changed swiftly. Faced with the reality of a direct attack on American forces, the Axis sympathizers disappeared from view, and the isolationists and disaffected minorities either participated in the war effort reluctantly or became persuaded that the world interest should now transcend their previous concerns.

What a difference this was from the American reaction to the Vietnam War, and how remarkable was this building of a national purpose with only two or three years of advance preparation on the part of President Roosevelt and his advisers. How could it happen that the American public would not revolt when a national conscription was imposed, ultimately drafting into military service every able-bodied male not the head of a family or engaged in a crucial occupation? How could people accept the strict allotment of meat, butter, and other foodstuffs; gasoline for cars; silk, nylon, and other clothing; and the absence of virtually all household products (like washers, refrigerators, and stoves) from the marketplace? For years, the American economy had been stalled by a crippling depression, with millions unemployed and unable to purchase even necessities. Now, the irony was that the extraordinary growth in manufacturing required to build the aircraft, tanks, ships, and other armaments, at a time when many men in the workforce had been taken off to military service, had brought full employment at high wages to everyone on the home front. For many women, this was their first opportunity for full-time, well-paid employment; for many African Americans, their first non-agricultural, urban employment. But with all this unprecedented prosperity, there was little to buy. And still, few complained.

The reason was that Americans were involved in following every step of the growing world conflict in their living rooms and at their workplaces, which led to a sense of national purpose. One of the most fundamental components of this exceptional national discipline was the role of the press and the other communications media in keeping the American public informed about the war, so that they could understand why they were being made to undergo such considerable sacrifices.

The people who did this reporting, in a variety of forms, constitute the subject of this book and of the exhibition that accompanies it. My colleague, Frederick S. Voss, has selected a representative group of these reporters and commentators to tell the fascinating story, and I have been greatly impressed by the authenticity and range of his scholarship in doing so. I have the advantage of my direct recollections of many of the characters he has included, and therefore this study has a special fascination for me.

I well recall evenings sitting around the radio in my family home in Detroit, listening to the direct broadcasts of the Blitz in London by Edward R. Murrow, the domestic evening radio news programs by H. V. Kaltenborn, with their detailed reports of German advances in the early stages of the Axis move across Europe and the German and Italian defeats as the tide began to turn. I remember the newspapers (with their frequent "Extra" editions and huge headlines) carrying dispatches from war correspondents who miraculously were able to wire stories back within hours or days of an event, *Life*'s amazing photographic coverage of field action and life behind the lines, cartoons from *Stars and Stripes* and *Yank* reprinted in the daily press and in books giving us a glimpse of the war from the soldier's ironic point of view, and the occasional special exhibitions of original paintings by war artists like David Friedenthal or Aaron Bohrod giving us at home a sense of the atmosphere and appearance of places we knew only as names in news stories.

Even though I was only in my early teens, I followed the action closely through the rough-and-ready maps published in the daily newspapers and in the brilliant cartography of Robert M. Chapin in *Time,* Richard Edes Harrison in *Life* and *Fortune,* and the other mapmakers who made us geographically literate so we could comprehend the interconnections of what we read about and heard about.

We needed this press coverage, because the mail we received from family members in the service was heavily censored. "V-Mail" letters (smudgy, reduced microfilms of letters handwritten on uniform-sized paper) invariably arrived with passages blacked out. Relations working in sensitive defense industries were cautioned to say little about the details of their work. Even portions of riverfronts and harbors were declared off-limits to unauthorized civilians, lest they reveal information about shipments of war materiel that might be useful to foreign agents. Nonetheless, by the time the war was over, we felt that we had followed every step of its action, seen every detail in the lives of the fighting men and women, and shared in all the information that could safely be made available.

Censorship could be carried too far, of course, and tended toward thought control on occasion. Recent articles have cited instances in which official reviewers refused to pass coverage that alluded to racial tension within the forces, required journalists to publish exaggerated tabulations of enemy losses, or inappropriately glorified high-ranking officers.

Despite these excesses, the consensus is that the system of censorship functioned honestly and appropriately, for the most part, and was respected by most of the working press at the time. Again, this is in striking contrast to the relationship between the military leadership and the working press in such recent conflicts as that in Kuwait.

Apart from the risk of losing their stories to censorship, very real hazards faced working journalists in World War II. At least 37 correspondents were killed, and another 112 wounded. Yet other reporters were imprisoned by the enemy, were forced to bail out of damaged aircraft into enemy territory, or had to survive under near-starvation conditions on the inhospitable jungle islands of the Pacific theater. Those who survived without serious damage to their bodies nevertheless carried the emotional imprint of their wartime experiences with them forever after.

The writers, combat artists, photographers, and editors named in the pages that follow are by no means the only ones who deserve mention. Since this is primarily the account of civilians reporting to civilians, photographers like Edward Steichen, Russell Lee, and Jack Delano, who did their work in uniform, are omitted, as are their writing colleagues who wrote exclusively in the service publications *Yank* and *Stars and Stripes.* If room had been available, it would have been useful to be reminded of the grit and ingenuity of the newsreel photographers, whose names were rarely as well known as the byline writers or syndicated cartoon artists, but whose work was fundamental in reporting the progress and feel of the war to those at home on a regular basis.

Another story only touched upon here deals with the opposition to the war, for the press was by no means a homogeneous cheering section. Apart from the occasional skeptical reporter or cynical cartoonist, there were publications edited by pacifists, by political opponents of the President, or by other disaffected groups; considerable effort was devoted to trying to control them or to nullify their effect, but they were present nonetheless. Undoubtedly, this is another subject, to be dealt with in another context, but it should be kept in mind as we read the pages that follow.

I cannot close without a word of thanks to the men and women who have shared their recollections and insights with us so generously, and have animated this study so considerably. Through their interviews (some on videotape) they have demonstrated how many components make up the free press that is so fundamental to the proper functioning of our nation. During the Second World War, the press faced a formidable challenge—to cover battles of unprecedented ferocity in widely scattered parts of the world, and to maintain the maximum of honesty and credibility while avoiding the immediate revelation of information that might have proved fatal to the military effort. That they succeeded as well as they did is testimony to the courage, the persistence, and the intelligence of the men and women of the Fourth Estate. That we still admire their articles, books, and pictures, and learn from them, attests to their skill and professionalism.

# ACKNOWLEDGMENTS

In compiling this book and the National Portrait Gallery exhibition of which it is a part, I have received help from many quarters, and no words can adequately express the full measure of gratitude owed to the scores of institutions and people that played a part in advancing this venture.

Chief among those who furthered the probe into the news coverage of World War II were a number of the individuals treated in the text of this book, and I offer deeply felt thanks to Daniel De Luce, Tom Lea, Carl Mydans, the late Leland Stowe, and the late Aaron Bohrod, all of whom readily answered my requests for help and information. I am also grateful to Bill Mauldin, Bernard Perlin, Robert St. John, the late William Shirer, and the late John Hersey for agreeing to record some of their wartime recollections on video-tape. The inconveniences that come with the intrusion of cameras and production crews into one's life are not always easy to bear, but no one could have borne the impositions more graciously than these five chroniclers of the war.

Warm thanks are due as well to staff of the many museums and archival facilities who assisted in my investigation into relevant collections housed at their institutions. Included in that number are: Frances Wilhoit of the journalism library at Indiana University; Margaret Goostray at Boston University's Mugar Library; Lucy Caswell at the Cartoon, Graphic, and Photographic Research Library at Ohio State University; Barbara Boyce at the Fletcher School of Law and Diplomacy, Tufts University; Sheryl Williams at the Kansas Collection of the University of Kansas; Antony Penrose at the Lee Miller Archives; Carolyn Davis at the Syracuse University Library; Michael Gonzales at the 45th Infantry Museum; and Rodney Brown at the War Museum.

I feel especially indebted to Mary Lou Gjernis, Joan Thomas, and Verne Schwartz, all of the United States Army Center of Military History, for repeatedly answering my requests for data on their collections so quickly and efficiently. At the same time, I am grateful to Ruth Ann Fredenthal and Michael Biddle, both the offspring of wartime field artists treated in this volume, for their willingness to make available some of the World War II drawings by their parents that are still in their possession. My warm appreciation also goes to Nancy Sorel for sharing with me her wide-ranging knowledge of female war correspondents.

Certain phases of this undertaking would not have been possible without special grants, and grateful acknowledgment of their generous financial support goes to the Smithsonian Women's Committee, the Smithsonian Special Exhibition Fund, and the Smithsonian Scholarly Research Fund.

The successful completion of the videotape interviews mentioned earlier depended heavily on three people: Lee Woodman of the Smithsonian's Office of Telecommunications, Robert Pierce of Robert Pierce Productions, Inc., and sound technician David Bartley. I am grateful to them not only for their professional expertise but also for their congeniality, which made this phase of the venture such a delight.

Finally, a vote of profound thanks is due to a number of colleagues at the National Portrait Gallery. For the National Portrait Gallery's curator of exhibitions, Beverly Cox, and her assistant curator, Claire Kelly, no praise can do justice to their invariably superb administration of this enterprise. Nor is it possible to properly thank the Gallery's publications officer, Frances Stevenson, and its editor, Dru Dowdy, for the part their able assistance and advice have played in making this publication a reality.

Frederick S. Voss

# LENDERS TO THE EXHIBITION

MICHAEL BIDDLE

BOSTON PUBLIC LIBRARY, MASSACHUSETTS

MUGAR MEMORIAL LIBRARY, BOSTON UNIVERSITY,
MASSACHUSETTS

PULITZER PRIZE OFFICE, COLUMBIA UNIVERSITY,
NEW YORK CITY

DANIEL DE LUCE

GEORGE EASTMAN HOUSE, ROCHESTER, NEW YORK

RUTH ANN AND ROBINSON FREDENTHAL

ESTATE OF JOHN HERSEY

SCHOOL OF JOURNALISM, INDIANA UNIVERSITY,
BLOOMINGTON

KANSAS COLLECTION, UNIVERSITY OF KANSAS
LIBRARIES, LAWRENCE

JOHN F. KENNEDY LIBRARY, BOSTON,
MASSACHUSETTS

LIBRARY OF CONGRESS, WASHINGTON, D.C.

GENERAL DOUGLAS MACARTHUR MEMORIAL,
NORFOLK, VIRGINIA

MOANA MCGLAUGHLIN-TREGASKIS THROUGH THE
MARINE CORPS MUSEUM, QUANTICO, VIRGINIA

MARINE CORPS MUSEUM, QUANTICO, VIRGINIA

NATIONAL ARCHIVES, WASHINGTON, D.C.

LIBRARY OF THE NATIONAL MUSEUM OF AMERICAN
ART AND NATIONAL PORTRAIT GALLERY,
SMITHSONIAN INSTITUTION, WASHINGTON, D.C.

NATIONAL PORTRAIT GALLERY, SMITHSONIAN
INSTITUTION, WASHINGTON, D.C.

CARTOON, GRAPHIC, AND PHOTOGRAPHIC ARTS
RESEARCH LIBRARY, THE OHIO STATE UNIVERSITY,
COLUMBUS

PRIVATE COLLECTIONS

HARRY RANSOM HUMANITIES RESEARCH CENTER,
THE UNIVERSITY OF TEXAS, AUSTIN

ROBERT ST. JOHN

ESTATE OF WILLIAM L. SHIRER

SOPHIA SMITH COLLECTION, SMITH COLLEGE,
NORTHAMPTON, MASSACHUSETTS

FRANK STANTON

STATE HISTORICAL SOCIETY OF WISCONSIN,
MADISON

SYRACUSE UNIVERSITY LIBRARY, NEW YORK

FLETCHER SCHOOL OF LAW AND DIPLOMACY, TUFTS
UNIVERSITY, MEDFORD, MASSACHUSETTS

UNITED STATES ARMY CENTER OF MILITARY HISTORY,
WASHINGTON, D.C.

THE WAR MUSEUM, NEW YORK CITY

# 1

# IN ON THE GROUND FLOOR

## REPORTING THE EARLY STAGES OF WAR

In the summer of 1939—as it became clear to all but the most myopic that Hitler's ranting about German territorial claims in Poland was about to take Europe into another major war—the American press was well prepared for covering this conflict, already being referred to as World War II. Twenty-five summers earlier, when Europe had faced a similar crisis, there had been only a handful of American correspondents scattered across the Continent, and when a young United Press reporter had on that occasion sent a 138-word telegram announcing a crucial development in the crisis, his employers had charged him with thoughtlessly frittering away their good money. This time, however, it was clearly going to be a case of "damn the costs" and "the more the merrier." By 1939 five major American dailies had generously staffed European offices of their own, all poised for covering the war when it came. Also girding themselves for that task were more than seven hundred reporters working in Europe for Associated Press, International News Service, and the once tightfisted United Press.

Taken by itself, the plenitude of correspondents augured well for thorough coverage of the war in the American press. At the same time, however, some members of the Fourth Estate worried that another factor would militate strongly against it. Recalling the often-wholesale news blackouts of World War I, they feared that with the onset of hostilities would come governmental efforts to curb war reportage and that, as *Time* put it, censorship soon "would reign over most of the British Isles and the Continent."[1]

To some extent, that fear proved justified. Shortly after Germany invaded Poland on September 1, an INS correspondent stationed in Warsaw cabled home, "Censorship toughest ever."[2] In France reporters' access to war-related developments was confined mainly to terse, uninformative army communiqués; in London correspondents encountered maddening delays in the filing of their stories as a result of having to pass every word they wrote through Great Britain's hastily established Ministry of Information; and in Germany all foreign press dispatches also were subjected to a censorship process. In the Soviet Union and Italy, America-bound news stories were not censored; nevertheless, their authors knew only too well that if their reporting deviated significantly from official interpretations of the war, they would simply be expelled.

Still, American reportage of the opening phases of war was often surprisingly compre-hensive and, taken altogether, represented the most thorough, accurate, and balanced news-paper coverage of a major war that the world had yet seen.

When news dispatches on the rumblings of war and the early stages of the war itself began flooding the press in this country, Americans in great numbers stood firmly by the conviction that this was a conflict that had nothing to do with them or United States inter-ests. For them, American involvement in the troubles of Europe was not only undesirable, it was totally unnecessary. The Europeans, ran the prevailing popular wisdom, had gotten themselves into this dreadful mess, and they would have to get themselves out of it.

It would be impossible to gauge exactly how all the news coverage of World War II's early phases affected these isolationist sentiments. One thing, however, seems reasonably certain: in bringing the realities of the war to the American public, the press contributed considerably to an erosion in that sentiment and gave birth to a recognition that, like it or not, this country would at some point have to become party to World War II.

Sigrid Schultz (detail). Atelier, Berlin, circa 1930. State Historical Society of Wisconsin, Madison. WHi(X3)47221

## SIGRID SCHULTZ

1893–1980

Petite, blond, and pretty, Sigrid Schultz had a look about her that was overwhelmingly feminine and perhaps even a little suggestive of frailty. Had she been a movie actress, no Hollywood producer would ever have dreamed of casting her in the role of a shrewd, hard-driving reporter. But that, in fact, was exactly what she was. A member of the *Chicago Tribune*'s German bureau since 1919 and director of its Berlin office since 1926, Schultz had by the mid-1930s acquired a reputation as one of the most astute press observers in Germany. When it came to ferreting out stories on Hitler's Nazi regime and its preparations for war, she was perhaps unmatched. Recalling their days together in Berlin, her friend and fellow reporter William Shirer later commented that of all the American journalists who witnessed the onset of World War II from within Germany, none "knew so much of what was going on behind the scene as did Sigrid Schultz."[3] Her *Tribune* boss, Colonel Robert McCormick, heartily agreed. In a note ordering a raise in her salary in the spring of 1939, he rationalized his generosity with the unequivocating declaration that "Schultz is our best correspondent."[4]

But a far more telling testimony to Schultz's journalistic expertise was the manifestation of Nazi hostility to her. Summoned to Gestapo offices on several occasions, where she was chastised for dispatches that cast the Third Reich in a less-than-flattering light, she had once been dubbed by Nazi leader Hermann Goering as the "dragon lady from Chicago."[5] At one point, Goering had even attempted to brand her as a spy by planting highly secret German military documents in her house; had Schultz not hastily burned these papers before they could be found in her possession, she might well have been incarcerated. If the animosity that Schultz aroused from time to time

This picture, taken at a Berlin press gala in the mid-1930s, leaves the impression that Sigrid Schultz is being somewhat flirtatious with Nazi propaganda minister Joseph Goebbels (*right*). In fact, Schultz recounted years later, she could not stand the oily Goebbels, and at the moment this picture was taken she was trying her best to avoid having to speak with him. American Ambassador William Dodd, standing to the left, "laughed his head off" when he saw the picture because he knew what Schultz had been trying to do. Unidentified photographer, circa 1935. State Historical Society of Wisconsin, Madison. WHi(X3)47222

within the Nazi establishment was any gauge, clearly she was doing something right.

One of Schultz's great talents lay in cultivating reliable insider news sources, and in 1938 and 1939 the information she gained from her extensive network of German contacts led to a succession of articles for the *Tribune* that revealed, in sometimes amazing detail, the workings and ambitions of the Third Reich. In the interest of protecting their author from possible reprisals from German authorities, the stories ran under the pseudonym John Dickson, and they carried false European datelines meant to suggest that Dickson was getting his information from sources outside German borders. It was a wise precaution. Running a broad gamut in terms of their subject matter, the articles offered convincing anecdotal proof of the ruthless oppression spawned by the Nazi regime and of its ever-more-ambitious military designs on much of the rest of Europe. If the Nazi establishment had known that Sigrid Schultz was the real author of these stories, it doubtless would have been risky for her to remain in Berlin.

Most of what Schultz reported in her Dickson series did not, strictly speaking, fall into the category of a journalistic exclusive. Rather, the main distinction of these articles was their often-graphic elaboration on German developments that other journalists were also reporting, though with less detail. But in July 1939, Schultz filed a story with the *Tribune* that must certainly rank among the most sig-

nificant and most overlooked scoops connected to the outbreak of World War II.

As Schultz recalled many years later, it all began with her German physician, Johannes Schmidt, whose patients included a number of well-placed Nazis who sometimes passed him tidbits of inside gossip. Among the items he picked up this way was the name of an astrologer whom Hitler sometimes consulted. When he passed this information on to Schultz, she arranged for an interview with the seer, who informed her that Hitler was contemplating a rapprochement with the Soviet Union.

Because Hitler had risen to power as an arch anticommunist and had always painted the Soviets as Germany's most dreaded enemy, the accuracy of this bit of news must initially have struck Schultz as somewhat dubious. On second thought, however, an alliance with the Soviets made perfect sense in the face of mounting evidence, in the spring and early summer of 1939, of Hitler's aggressive designs on Poland. For the European power most interested in thwarting those designs, and best positioned geographically to do so, was the Soviet Union. So it was only logical that the Third Reich's strategists should be regarding an amiable relationship with the Soviets as a highly desirable, if not essential, ingredient in its rapidly gelling plans for eastward expansion.

And sure enough, as Schultz tested the validity of the seer's observations in this matter, she began encountering an assortment of rumors and facts indicating that a

## SIGRID SCHULTZ SPOTS SIGNS OF GERMAN-SOVIET RAPPROCHEMENT
*CHICAGO TRIBUNE*, JULY 13, 1939

The high command of the armed forces of Germany no longer is aware of the exact plans of Fuehrer Hitler.

Three officers were arrested in June for repeating statements made to them by Hitler. Since then he has merely issued orders to his high command without discussing the details of his plans. The result is that a nervousness grips the dictator's own men.

If one talks to persons who have been in conference with Hitler recently and if one studies developments behind the official curtain, it is possible to get a clear picture of the aims and aspirations of Hitler.

The outstanding factor is: He has a New World Enemy No. 1.

Communism, soviet Russia and Dictator Stalin were called the arch enemies of civilization when Hitler was advancing toward supreme power. Hatred of communism and the faith of the bourgeois that he would save them from communism helped him become master of Germany.

Today England is being proclaimed as World Enemy No. 1. She is accused of usurping the rights of small nations, of opposing Germany's "right to be the first power in the world."

Hatred of England is simmering or blazing in Japan, India, Arabia, Africa, Ireland, Russia, and England's ally, France. It is being fanned systematically by Nazi agents throughout the world.

Hitler, it is said, hopes to use this hatred to establish Germany as the most powerful nation in the world, the same as he used the German citizen's hatred of communism to establish his rule in Germany. . . .

. . . . Friendship with soviet Russia, or at least an understanding with her, can prove

German-Soviet entente was quite possibly in the offing. Accordingly, she was soon at work on a lengthy Dickson article strongly suggesting that by June 1939 German diplomatic efforts were consciously aiming toward that goal.

When Schultz's story appeared in the *Chicago Tribune* on July 13, however, it apparently did not attract the considered attention that it deserved. As a result, when Germany and the Soviet Union signed their mutual nonaggression pact on

a powerful weapon in Germany's campaign "to force England to her knees," diplomatic sources declare. . . .

Statements made by Hitler's and Von Ribbentrop's inner circles indicate there is much truth in various assertions that Stalin is eager for an understanding with Hitler. When William Strang, special British envoy, arrived in Moscow, usually well informed Nazi circles said their friends in Moscow "had laid mines which were bound to explode and ruin all British efforts" to conclude a mutual aid pact with Moscow.

Plans for soviet-German cooperation along economic lines are under discussion in Moscow. Political negotiators also are there. They include German industrialists traveling under false names. How far the negotiators will get is another question. But even the start of negotiations is considered a tremendous weapon in the hands of the dictators, who, it is said, are eager to scare capitalism and democracy. The newest toast in high Hitler-Guard circles is: "To our new ally, Russia."

The Germans figure that the English are so terrified of the possible formation of a soviet-German bloc that Prime Minister Chamberlain and Foreign Secretary Viscount Halifax will again go to Germany and offer all the concessions the Germans want. If the British fail to respond to the threat, the Germans argue that they can still get enough raw materials and money out of Russia to make the deal worth while. . . .

The Nazis admit an understanding with Stalin would discredit Hitler's claim that he is a crusader against communism.

"If Hitler says the wicked Red soviets are no longer Red nor wicked, the Germans will accept his word," diplomatic students declare. "The patience of a German fully equals that of the Russian peasant."

August 23, thus opening the way for Germany's unopposed march into Poland and the onset of World War II nine days later, announcement of the agreement left most of the world in a state of "stunned surprise."[6] One of the few not succumbing to bewildered shock, of course, was Sigrid Schultz.

Schultz remained in Berlin following the invasion of Poland and covered World War II from there for nearly a year and a half. Ever-tightening German censorship,

Although she detested the Nazis, Schultz was too good a reporter not to cultivate cordial relationships with some of them. Among the first Nazis she singled out for that honor was Hermann Goering, who sent her this telegram wishing her a happy New Year for 1932. One reason she picked Goering was that she had heard that he was one of the few Nazis with decent table manners. State Historical Society of Wisconsin, Madison. WHi(X3)47224

however, made it increasingly difficult for her to report the war with any candor, and in late January 1941 she was on her way back to the United States in search of some respite from Nazi news control. But by summer she was ready to return to Berlin, and in August she applied for a visa, only to find that once rid of the "dragon lady from Chicago," the Germans did not want her back.

In the short term, Schultz may have considered the Germans' rejection of her visa request a disappointing setback. But perhaps it was all for the best. Shortly after the United States entered the war some three months later, she learned from newspaper friends, who had heard it from a German source, that had she been back at her *Tribune* desk in Berlin, she might be facing deep trouble. According to the German source, a Third Reich authority had decreed that in the event of war with America, Schultz would be excluded from the exchange of nationals that customarily takes place between warring nations at the outbreak of hostilities. Instead, she was to be detained indefinitely. As likely as not, the story was baseless. Even so, it was one Nazi rumor, the truth of which Schultz was perfectly happy not to be exploring firsthand.

## LELAND STOWE

1899–1994

In the summer of 1933, the *New York Herald Tribune*'s Pulitzer Prize–winning foreign correspondent Leland Stowe arrived in Berlin to fill in for a couple of months for a vacationing *Herald Tribune* reporter. Stowe, whose regular beat was Paris, had volunteered for this temporary duty because he was curious to see how Germany was faring under its new chancellor, Nazi party leader Adolf Hitler. What he found shocked him. Having come to power January 30, Hitler had in less than two months managed to persuade the German Reichstag to invest him with dictatorial powers, and by summer Germany was well on its way to becoming a rabidly militaristic police state hell-bent on establishing its dominance over much of Europe. At least that was the way Stowe saw it, and before long, he concluded that this was a story in urgent need of telling.

As a result, by the time he was ready to return to Paris, he had collated a mass of economic, social, and political evidence for a series of ten news stories on current trends in Germany that in his view could point to but one conclusion: Hitler's often-stated claim that he wanted only peaceful coexistence between Germany and its neighbors was a lie, and he was instead already looking to the day when his country would claim dominion over Austria and "large slices" of Central Europe. Moreover, Stowe was convinced that this expansion represented only the starting point for Hitler's ambitions, and Germany's new leader would not rest satisfied until "Prussian culture" held sway over "all of Europe."[7] For Stowe, that could mean only one conclusion: within ten years, and probably a lot sooner, Europe would be engulfed in a war every bit as devastating as the one that ended in 1918.

In hindsight, Stowe's analysis of what was going on in Germany seems to bela-

Leland Stowe. Unidentified photographer, circa 1941. Courtesy estate of Leland Stowe

bor the obvious. When he finished his German articles in the fall of 1933, however, and sent them off for publication in the *Herald Tribune,* they represented one of the first comprehensive attempts by a journalist to lay out the disturbing implications of Hitler's rise. As such, one would have thought, as indeed Stowe did, that the *Herald Tribune* would have been mightily pleased to print them. But although Stowe's credibility as a clear-eyed and thoughtful observer was by now well established, his editors back in New York found the conclusions drawn in these pieces far too alarmist for their tastes, and they decided not to run them.

Nevertheless, the articles did finally see the light of day, when a London publisher decided to bring them out in book form under the title *Nazi Germany Means War.* But even with that attention-grabbing title, the volume went largely unread both in the British Isles and the United States. Aside from a mere handful of reviewers who congratulated him on his thoughtful analysis, Stowe had raised a warning that very few in late 1933 were interested in heeding.

But whereas his prophecies of war caused nary a discernible ripple, the same could not be said of Stowe's reportage of the war itself. When the *Herald Tribune* informed him at the outbreak of World War II that he was too old to serve as one of the paper's war correspondents, Stowe wasted no time in finding a newspaper that did not harbor such biases toward staff members who happened to be forty. By

Pictured here is the occupation of Oslo, Norway by German troops in April 1940, the story of which represented one of Leland Stowe's most impressive journalistic accomplishments. Unidentified photographer, 1940. Still Picture Branch, National Archives, Washington, D.C.

mid-September 1939, he had quit the *Herald Tribune* and was on his way to Europe as a frontline correspondent for the *Chicago Daily News*. His former employer's loss was, without doubt, the *Daily News*'s very substantial gain. By 1943 he had covered the war from the vantage point of seven different national armies, weathered bombing attacks by five different air forces, and filed his dispatches from no fewer than forty-four countries and colonies on four continents. More to the point, Stowe had secured a reputation as one of the war's most capable and intrepid reporters.

Stowe's most significant coup as a war correspondent occurred in April of 1940. Early that month, not totally recovered from the exhaustion resulting from his recent coverage of the Soviets' winter invasion of Finland, he decided on the spur of the moment to cancel his plans to go to Latvia for a little rest and instead pay a working visit to Oslo, Norway. Exactly what sort of news story he thought he was going to find in that Scandinavian capital is not altogether clear. But whatever it was, it was a far cry from the one he actually encountered. He arrived in Oslo on April 4, and five days later began witnessing the first stages in Germany's surprise invasion of Norway. For many weeks thereafter, his dispatches served as the single most reliable news source on the fall of that country into Nazi hands. By early May it was widely thought, within American newspaper circles, that this Norway coverage made Stowe almost a shoo-in for his second Pulitzer Prize.

The Pulitzer never materialized. Nevertheless, Stowe's chronicle of Norway's collapse did underscore the ineptitude of Great Britain's tardy, ill-planned, and ultimately disastrous attempt to aid the Norwegians in staving off their German invaders. In doing so, he believed that he was performing "just about the most important and constructive" service of his professional life, and behind his frankness was a hope that it might somehow shock the British government into adopting more effective strategies in its war on German aggression.[8] By mid-May of 1940, there was at least one indication that Stowe may have achieved that purpose: As portions of his Norwegian stories found their way into the British press, they inspired a wave of indignation that contributed to the political demise of Prime Minister Neville Chamberlain.

## ROBERT ST. JOHN
BORN 1902

In the summer of 1938, as events in Europe and Asia moved the world ever closer to global conflict, Robert St. John was living out a pastoral fantasy that was not uncommon among reporters such as himself. Or at least part of it. A seasoned urban journalist whose credentials included a stint with the Associated Press and an exposé on gangster Al Capone that had left him lying brutally beaten in a suburban Chicago gutter, St. John had decided in 1933 that he had had quite enough of meeting daily press deadlines. At age thirty-one, he had retired with his wife, Eda, to a farm in New Hampshire. His intention was to earn a modest living from agricultural pursuits and in his leisure, which he assumed would be ample, compose the great plays and novels that he had long dreamed of writing. The reality, however, did not exactly square with the original vision. Although he managed to scratch out an acceptable living through such pursuits as raising chickens and manufacturing replicas of an early American snuffbox for tourists, he soon found himself with little time or energy left over for fulfilling his literary ambitions. Even so, St. John was quite content with his rustic existence, and many years later he looked back on his New Hampshire venture as one of the happiest periods of his life.

But the bucolic idyll did not altogether kill off St. John's once-healthy appetite for journalistic adventure, and when a friend from his days at AP, reporter Frank Gervasi, paid him a visit in the late summer of 1938, his dormant hankering for chasing down news was suddenly reawakened. As St. John later recalled it, Gervasi first came upon him while he was picking blueberries, and once the two men had settled down to renewing their acquaintance, Gervasi had wasted no time in reproving his host for hiding away when he could be reporting the coming of war in Europe. That Hitler's aggressive inclinations and ambitious rearmament programs for Germany were causing tension on the Continent was known to St. John. Nevertheless, during the past five years, staying abreast of the latest in international developments had not been a priority for him, and when Gervasi predicted that by September 1939 Hitler's quest for *Lebensraum* would plunge much of Europe into war, St. John was taken aback. More important, he was hooked. By the end of the visit, St. John and Gervasi had agreed to meet in Paris the following summer, where they would team up to write a syndicated column on the mounting European crisis.

As a result, over the next year or so, St. John's energies were focused on raising enough cash to finance boat passages to Europe for himself and his wife and, at the same time, assure them of ample funds for their first several months abroad. By the coming of summer in 1939, with that goal nearly accomplished, Robert and Eda St. John were looking forward to trading the peaceful rural simplicity of New Hamp-

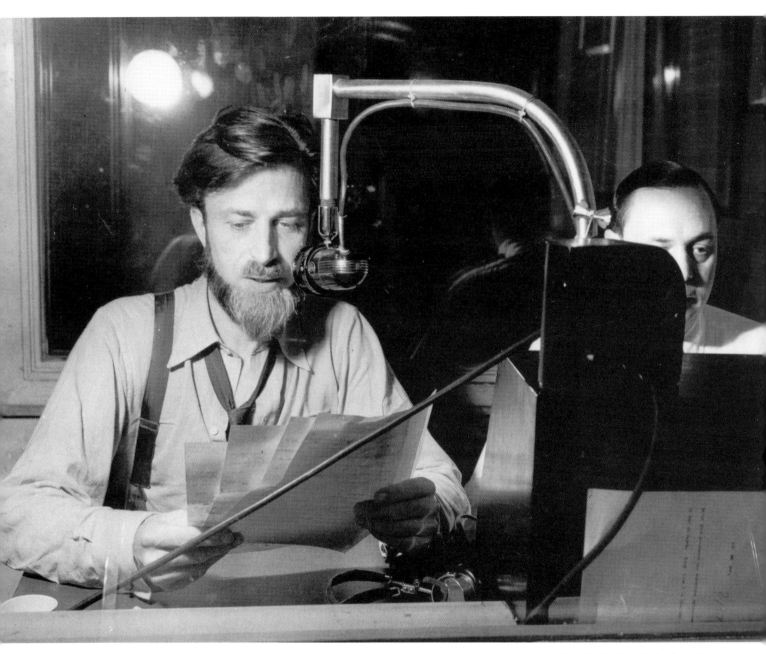

Shortly after returning home from Eastern Europe in 1941, St. John took a job with NBC as a news commentator and for much of the war did his broadcasting from England.

In the picture here, St. John is seated in a studio in New York. The day is August 14, 1945; the time is 7:05 P.M.; and thanks to a shrewd guess about the teletype signals he

has just heard in NBC's newsroom, St. John is reporting the surrender of Japan roughly twenty seconds ahead of his radio network competition. About an hour

later, he had the distinction of reporting the end of World War II on a newfangled invention called television. Unidentified photographer, 1945. Courtesy Robert St. John

shire for the cosmopolitan and decidedly more troubled atmosphere of Europe.

There was only one problem: Gervasi, having received a job offer from *Collier's* that he could not refuse, had by then informed St. John that the plans for their projected partnership were off. But St. John was far too committed to becoming a foreign correspondent to let that deter him, and he was soon on his way to New York, hoping to land a European assignment with one of the country's wire services. Unfortunately, aside from the vanity-wounding observation made by several potential employers that, at age thirty-seven, he was "a little too old" for the rigors of overseas reporting, this job search yielded nothing.[9] Nevertheless, St. John's determination to return to journalism remained undiminished. By mid-August, with Europe on the verge of war, just as Gervasi had predicted, and his New Hampshire farmhouse safely boarded up, St. John was bound for France, confident that, his advancing senility notwithstanding, a job would finally turn up.

And indeed one did.

Arriving in Paris on August 28, St. John quickly surmised that his best chances for employment lay considerably farther east, and at about noontime on September 1, he walked into the offices of Associated Press in Budapest, Hungary. On this first full day in the Hungarian capital, however, he was not intending to ask for a job. Rather, he had gone to AP in search of a fellow American who might be interested in joining him and his wife for lunch and who also knew enough Hungarian to help them decipher the menu. Instead of a dining companion, he found pandemonium. Unbeknownst to him, Hitler's armies had early that morning marched into Poland; the European phase of World War II had begun; and AP's Budapest office was frantically trying to do its part in putting together the story. Somehow in the midst of this chaos, St. John made it known that he was a newsman, and within minutes he was being enlisted to assist the AP staffers in their efforts to collate the particulars on what was happening in Poland.

St. John never got his lunch. But he did get a job, and over the next several weeks, because Budapest's geographical location gave the AP offices there a distinct edge in obtaining up-to-date stories on the progress of Germany's Polish invasion, he had a central role in informing the rest of the world about it.

This, however, was only the beginning. In the next twenty months or so, the Axis alliance, with Germany in the lead, would, through a combination of diplomatic negotiation, infiltration, intimidation, and out-and-out armed force, succeed in imposing its control over all of Central Europe and the Balkans. And among those witnessing this turn of events was the one-time farmer from New Hampshire.

As Hungary, Romania, Bulgaria, Albania, Yugoslavia, and finally Greece fell under Axis sway either as puppet states or occupied territories, St. John, in a good many respects, relished his bird's-eye view of this development. After all, this was what he had come to Europe for, and like any reporter worthy of the name, he took considerable satisfaction when the stories he scrambled after drew compliments from AP headquarters in New York.

But the road to professional satisfaction was not an easy one, and doubtless there was more than one occasion when St. John could not understand why he had succumbed to Frank Gervasi's urging that he come to Europe. Among his more routine difficulties were the logistics of getting his stories out in a corner of the world where he sometimes seemed to be blocked at every turn by government censorship and communication facilities that were rapidly deteriorating in the face of Axis takeovers. Ultimately St. John became quite resourceful in overcoming this problem. But even when he succeeded in sending out a dispatch, that, too, could be as troubling as when he had failed. While covering the fall of Romania and Bulgaria, for example, the slants taken in several of his stories resulted in orders for his immediate expulsion, and it was only thanks to some fortunately timed surges in the prevailing political chaos of those two countries that the orders were never carried out.

But the difficulties encountered in Romania and Bulgaria were small compared to those he met with in Yugoslavia in the early spring of 1941, as that country mounted its last-ditch armed struggle to resist Hitler's attempts to force it into the Axis orbit. Here, without doubt, was the most dramatic news story that he had yet encountered; unfortunately a combination of government censorship and ruptures in the normal lines of communication to the outside world prevented him from sending it out. The one compensation for that professional disappointment was that St. John did not have much time to brood about it. By then he knew, through his network of sources, that some of his recent reporting had strongly offended the Germans. And although as a reporter from a neutral country he was technically protected from any reprisal, he feared that things would not go well for him should he find himself within German lines. Consequently, as a German victory in Yugoslavia became inevitable, St. John's main preoccupation was finding a way out of this war-ravaged country. By mid-April, having reached Yugoslavia's Dalmatian coast barely one step ahead of the Germans, he and three other reporters were on a disturbingly unseaworthy twenty-foot sardine boat, arduously making their way through the choppy seas of the Adriatic toward Greece and hoping that they could make their destination before running afoul of Axis warships or mines.

With the help of a convivial sixty-year-old Serbian fisherman, later killed by German strafing, that hope was fulfilled. But Greece was not the safer haven that St. John would have wished. Besieged by Italian and German forces, the country was on the verge of becoming yet another victim of Axis aggression. For St. John it was largely a repeat of his Yugoslavia experience: Thanks to the local chaos, he found himself once again eyewitness to one of the most dramatic news stories of the moment, which he was unable to file; and he was too concerned with surviving to anguish much about that professional failure.

Eventually, though not before being wounded in a German air attack, St. John did find safety from the Nazi juggernaut via the British navy, which picked him up in the Peloponnesus and evacuated him to Egypt. There he at last began grinding out dispatches on some of what he had just seen. But even then he was unable to report the full story, and when, for example, British military censors in Cairo saw his frank account of the disastrous British effort to aid the Greeks in repelling the Axis invasion, they wasted no time in excising any discussion of the staggering human losses incurred by that failed expedition.

Nevertheless, the frustrations of having to keep the story of what he had just witnessed in the Balkans under wraps finally did come to an end. Soon after returning to the United States in the summer of 1941, St. John, with fragments of a German shell still lodged in his leg, retreated to a New York hotel room to produce a day-by-day chronicle of the collapse of Yugoslavia and Greece. The result was a best-selling book entitled *From the Land of the Silent People,* which at its publication early in 1942 was hailed by one critic as one of the "most distinguished" pieces of "frontline reporting" to yet come out of the war.[10] For a man who only a few years earlier had been told he was over the hill, that was no mean accomplishment.

THE WEEK-END ARGUS MAGAZINE SECTION — SATURDAY, JULY 5, 1941.

*Robert St. John, the American War Correspondent, tells of his Remarkable Adventure in the Adriatic Sea*

# THREE MEN in a BOAT
### —To Say Nothing of the Fish!

## My Escape From Yugoslavia

*By Robert St. John—as told in an interview with Weldon Broughton*

## Sailing Through the Italian Fleet

After his escape from the Balkans, Robert St. John made his way back to the United States via Cape Town, South Africa, where the local newspaper turned him into a momentary celebrity with this account of his flight from the Nazis in 1941. Courtesy Robert St. John

# 2

# THE NATION'S SECURITY VS. THE RIGHT TO KNOW

In early September 1943, Office of War Information chief Elmer Davis met with President Roosevelt to complain that the public was being shielded from the war's less pleasant realities for no good reason. Among the things he wanted was a lifting of the ban on publication of pictures of dead American soldiers. Arguing that being too Pollyannaish would lead to an unhealthy public cynicism, Davis won his point. Shortly after the meeting, *Life* published this photograph of three dead American soldiers on a Southwest Pacific beach—one of the first such news pictures to appear in the American press. George Strock (lifedates unknown), for *Life* magazine, 1943. © Time Warner Inc.

The First Amendment to the United States Constitution guarantees the freedom of the press, which by and large means that no government authority can prohibit the country's purveyors of news from reporting on events of the day or expressing their opinions and speculations on the meanings of those events. This freedom is one of the most carefully guarded institutions in America and is viewed as one of the most sacred tenets of its democracy. Crises, however, have periodically arisen where a rigorously observed freedom of the press has collided with what was deemed to be the national interest, and when the right to report the unvarnished truth of events has promised to deepen the crisis at hand, government has sometimes curtailed the full exercise of that right. World War II was one such occasion. Shortly after America's entry as an active participant in that conflict in December 1941, the American press found itself noticeably hampered in carrying out its daily mission of informing its readers on the war-related news. This is not to say that what ensued was an officially mandated wholesale blackout of the war's happenings. What it did mean, however, was that following Congress's approval of Franklin Roosevelt's request for a war on Germany and Japan, the federal government lost no time in establishing regulations and mechanisms designed to limit and to a large extent channel the war's news coverage.

The rationales for this departure from freedom of the press were not difficult to understand, and generally speaking, journalists and the news-consuming public alike were sympathetic to them. After all, with the country engaged in global war, it seemed eminently clear that widely published detailed accounts on such matters as Allied battlefront movements, weapons development, and setbacks in our own war efforts could well reach our enemies and aid them immeasurably in determining their next moves against us. Further-

As this cartoon published three days after Japan's attack on Pearl Harbor indicates, it was clear from the moment America entered World War II that newspapers would have to live with censorship. The situation addressed in the cartoon is the fact that Secretary of War Henry Stimson and Secretary of the Navy Frank Knox were not being candid about the true extent of American losses at Pearl Harbor. So far, the government line was that only one "old" battleship and a destroyer had been sunk when, in truth, the damage to the country's Pacific defenses had been devastating. Clifford Berryman (1869–1949), 1941. Pen and ink on paper, 34.3 x 36.8 cm (13½ x 14½ in.). Prints and Photographs Division, Library of Congress, Washington, D.C.

more, there was the question of America's own wartime morale. If the press were to indulge too freely in airing items casting the country's war efforts in a negative light, the collective will to fight the war to a victorious end might become dangerously weakened. In short, the consensus both in and out of government, civilian as well as military, was that a temporary circumscribing of one of the Constitution's most cherished guaranteed freedoms was a small price to pay for national survival in this moment of peril.

The government's entry into the business of news control took several forms. First, there was the Office of Censorship, headed by the Associated Press's former executive editor, Byron Price. Formally established in January 1942, this was a purely civilian enterprise, charged with monitoring war-related news emanating from within the United States proper. Then there was military censorship, under which the various branches of the armed

This is one of many posters produced by the Office of War Information to sell the American people on the need for curbing the normally free flow of information in wartime. How effective the posters were is not known. The fact is, however, that on the whole the country accepted the curbs without much complaint. Stevan Dohanos (born 1907), circa 1943. Color halftone poster, 71 x 52.1 cm (27¹⁵⁄₁₆ x 20½ in.). Poster Collection, Library of Congress, Washington, D.C.

service claimed the right to curb the release of news about their combat activities that was deemed to be potentially harmful to their fighting effectiveness. Finally, there was the Office of War Information, headed by ex-reporter and radio commentator Elmer Davis, which was meant to serve as a major clearinghouse for war news and which, in consultation with the military and other government agencies, was to play a significant role in determining what news ought to be aired and when.

The divisions of responsibility within this triad of government-sponsored news control to some extent overlapped, and there was often difficulty in knowing who had the final say in specific matters. Still, on the whole, the system worked reasonably well, and although stories sometimes found their way into the press that seemed to jeopardize the country's wartime security, such leakage generally had no significant negative effect on the war effort. Moreover, the members of the press, despite their deeply ingrained eagerness for a good, complete, and honest story, generally grew accustomed to censorship and accepted it as a temporary fact of their working life. That did not mean that they were always in agreement with the definition of national security that given censors applied in cutting up or reshaping their stories, nor did it mean that they never protested the suppression of one of their pieces. In fact, there was a fair amount of press grumbling—both individually and collectively—along those lines. Nevertheless, as much infected with wartime patriotic fervor as anyone, they by and large acquiesced to the governmental monitoring of their profession.

## BYRON PRICE
### 1901–1976

As a career journalist and occupant of one of the top positions at Associated Press, Byron Price was not at all sympathetic to the notion of limiting the free flow of news. In his professional lexicon, "every act" of press censorship contradicted "the democratic creed," and he was more than a little inclined to agree with the AP em-ployee who had declared to him shortly after Pearl Harbor that a censor was undoubtedly "the lowest form of human existence."[1] Nevertheless, Price was enough of a realist to see that the security demands of a nation engaged in full-scale war necessitated some kind of censorship. As a result, when Franklin Roosevelt summoned him to Washington a few days after Pearl Harbor to discuss the possibility of his heading up an office of civilian censorship, he did not dismiss the proposition

Byron Price. Unidentified photographer, not dated. Still Picture Branch, National Archives, Washington, D.C.

# AMERICAN NEWSPAPER PUBLISHERS ASSOCIATION

## 370 LEXINGTON AVENUE
## NEW YORK

CENSORSHIP BULLETIN No. 3                                    January 27, 1942.

### (Not for Publication)

TO PUBLISHERS AND EDITORS OF ALL DAILY NEWSPAPERS:

### SUGGESTIONS FOR CONSIDERATION OF EDITORS.

One editor has suggested that newspapers might well consider abandoning articles which idealize the Japanese psychology about suicide. The point is made that by idealizing this psychology we are selling our own people, particularly our soldiers, the idea that the Japs are a tougher customer than anyone else and would be harder to lick because he does not mind getting killed.

Another person has suggested that editors be careful about the use of pictures from their morgues in connection with current news developments. It happens that the person who brought up this point is in the picture business himself and has an understanding of the impact of pictures. He illustrated by saying that a picture of a battleship taken some time back and used in connection with a current story, might reveal some information as to structure, type, etc., which would be highly valuable to the enemy. Of course, others say that if the picture has been **used heretofore** the chances are that it is already in the hands of the enemy.

---

out of hand. In fact, he was quite agreeable to it, provided that the soon-to-be-born Office of Censorship was to be founded on certain rigorously observed premises. One—wisely anticipating that there might be high officials within the government who would favor more stringent brands of censorship than he—Price insisted that he would be responsible only to the President and that, save for an overriding of his decisions by FDR, he would otherwise have a free hand in devising his agency's policies. Two, he wanted the system of press censorship to be in large degree voluntary, which meant that one of Censorship's main tasks would be to persuade, rather than force, the country's newspapers, magazines, and radio stations into following his office's guidelines for curbing news.

Roosevelt had little trouble in accepting these ground rules. So, by early January 1942, the Office of Censorship, with Price as its director, had established its hastily improvised and cramped headquarters in the postal department. By mid-month it was issuing its first pamphlet setting out the guidelines by which it hoped the news media would, with only a minimum of active coercion, abide in determining what war-related news was fit to print and what was not.

At the heart of these guidelines was a single question that Price wanted the press to ask itself in reviewing every story for publication: "Is this information I would like to have if I were the enemy?"[2] If the answer was a clear and obvious "no," then naturally the story in question could run; if "yes," it should not; and if "maybe," the

In the first section of this January 27, 1942, bulletin from the Office of Censorship, the nation's press was advised to play down traits commonly attributed to Japanese soldiers that might make them seem unbeatable. Not mentioned was the reasoning behind this advice, namely that emphasis on the Japanese soldier's fighting virtues could erode confidence in the Allied cause. Don Anderson Papers, State Historical Society of Wisconsin, Madison. WHi(X3)45462

editor, Censorship's four-page pamphlet urged, should feel free to bring the story to the Office of Censorship for advice.

Although the fundamental operant question in the country's new censorship system was readily understandable, the full range of news topics on which it might have some bearing was not. Through its first pamphlet and subsequent revisions of it, the Office of Censorship thus enumerated for the news industry the many types of information that it should refrain from airing. Among the more obvious kinds were such things as troop movements and precise locations of army and navy installations. In addition, however, there were topics that Censorship deemed sensitive but that most editors might not have been mindful of unless they had been specifically pointed out. There was, for example, weapons production, a matter where the press was discouraged from calling attention to even the most rudimentary—often already commonly known—facts about the country's armaments factories lest those facts attract the attention of Axis saboteurs. And because knowledge of winds and storm fronts might influence an enemy's plan for attacking the United States proper or Allied shipping off its coasts, daily weather reports also fell into the censorable category, and newspapers were asked to sharply curtail their routine coverage of the weather.

Price was correct when, at the outset of his venture into censorship, he sensed that there were sure to be officials in wartime Washington pressing for more all-encompassing censorship policies than he and his staff were inclined to impose. Indeed, one school of thought held that news control should go beyond the realm of sensitive factual information to embrace editorial opinion as well. The argument for doing so focused on the premise that unchecked editorial criticism of the war's conduct could conceivably imperil collective support for the war. Price could see that this was a hazard, and he could live with the eventual government shutdown of a few fringe publications whose professions of antipathy for the war were virulent in the extreme. By and large, however, the notion of hampering the free trafficking in journalistic opinion offended his democratic sensibilities, and he steadfastly guarded against any larger attempt to stifle the more normal brands of wartime criticism.

Price liked to call his version of censorship "the Voice of the Dove," and his friendly and unintimidating methods for urging the press to practice a system of mostly voluntary self-scrutiny worked pretty well.[3] There were, to be sure, a good many times when the Office of Censorship had to chastise various journalists for violating its guidelines, and in a few instances he even had to call First Lady Eleanor Roosevelt to task for airing items in her syndicated column, "My Day," that represented minor infractions of those guidelines. After one such occasion, one wag ventured the opinion that Price deserved a Distinguished Service Medal for accomplishing something that Franklin Roosevelt himself could never do: He had "told Mrs. Roosevelt not to talk so much" and had moreover obtained "her promise to comply with his admonition."[4]

But Price's success with Mrs. Roosevelt was only a humorous sidelight to the significantly larger testament to Censorship's effectiveness. For, thanks to the agency's velvet-gloved techniques in news control, the United States had managed, with comparatively few exceptions, to strike an astonishingly healthy balance between allowing the press to report the war's progress and keeping information potentially helpful to the enemy under wraps.

What was more, the Office of Censorship had accomplished this end while still retaining the general goodwill of the press, and among the most telling indica-tions of that was the warm praise that came Byron Price's way at war's end. One editor in Detroit congratulated him on having presided over the "most efficiently, the most rationally" run organization in all of wartime Washington, and another assured him that he was leaving office with "the whole-hearted admiration of every newsman" with whom he had dealt.[5] Some correspondents had grown so comfortable with Price's news-monitoring regime that, even as Censorship began promptly closing its operations following the Japanese surrender in August 1945, they continued to seek its advice on the handling of stories. When one correspondent was told that this was no longer necessary, she asked, "But where will we go now to get our stories cleared?"[6]

No head of a war-created bureau moved more quickly to close down his operation at war's end than did Byron Price. When word of Japanese surrender reached Washington on August 14, 1945, he wasted not a minute in gaining presidential consent for shutting Censorship. By mid-afternoon the next day, the deed was done, and Price, who had always distrusted his censor's mission, was happily taping an out-of-business sign on his office door. Unidentified photographer, 1945. AP/Wide World Photos

## ADMIRAL ERNEST KING
1878–1956

Byron Price's Office of Censorship proved to be a model of self-restraint in carrying out its news-limiting mandate. Others involved in wartime censorship, however, did not, and in its efforts to protect the nation's security from potentially harmful news leaks, the armed services often defined "potentially harmful" far more broadly than Price ever did. The result was that news emanating from military press offices both at the front and in Washington was not always as candid as it might have been. There were, for example, times when the full extent of Allied failures and losses was kept out of public print, not because disclosure might help the enemy in playing to Allied weaknesses, but simply because it reflected negatively on the Allied performance. In other instances, bona fide triumphs were unnecessarily exaggerated. Most astounding, in retrospect, the history of the war's press coverage even includes examples—most notably the devastating Japanese naval setback at the Battle of Midway in June 1942—where the real extent of Allied victory went underreported for many months, thanks largely to armed-service reticence in publicizing it.

Among the individuals who were responsible for the military's sometimes painfully tight clamps on war news was Admiral Ernest King. Appointed commander in chief of all naval operations in December 1941, this crusty, harsh-mannered officer once inspired his daughter to declare him "the most even tempered man in the navy" because, she said, "he is always in a rage."[7] When King became commander in chief, one of the first things that he made clear to his civilian boss, Secretary of the Navy Frank Knox, was that no one should expect him to give press conferences. So saying, King gave telling indication of the tone he intended to set with regard to the navy's relations with the press. As far as he was concerned, the less the newspapers knew about his branch's wartime progress the better. As a result, it was soon making the rounds in Washington that there was but one story that Admiral King deemed acceptable for release: It would be disseminated to the press at war's end, and assuming that all went as hoped, it would announce the fact that the Allies had won.

That was a bit of an exaggeration, however. Although King was more distrustful than most about what he once publicly called the news media's lack of "discrimination in regard to giving 'aid and comfort' to the enemy," he did grudgingly recognize the need to provide the press with something to say about his service's contribution to the war effort.[8] To that end, he often personally oversaw the drafting and editing of the navy's news releases. Nevertheless, this personal attention was driven less by a desire to be informative than it was by an unabating preoccupation with limiting the scope of the releases. Throughout much of the war, he was the despair of not just the news-seeking press but also of many government officials, who worried that his extreme secrecy would engender public cynicism and severely damage the navy's credibility.

Not surprisingly, King's treatment of journalists generated some indignant protests, among them a letter from the country's three major news services complaining that the military in general, and the navy in particular, were not keeping the public "adequately informed about the war."[9] For the most part, such chiding failed to reform King's uncooperative ways. Moreover, he also remained un-

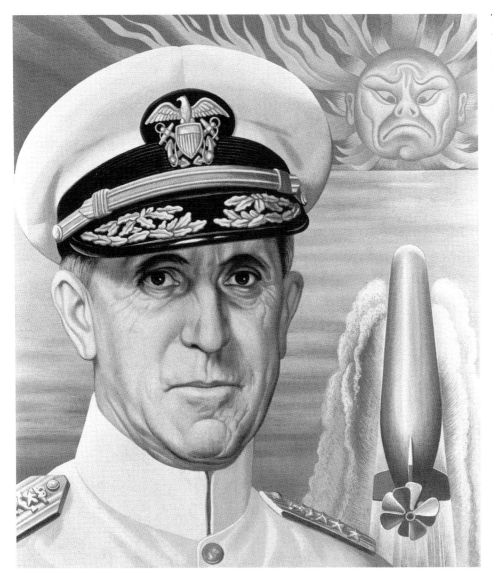

This image of Admiral King was painted for a *Time* cover story that appeared in December 1942. The picture, however, was never used. Among the tidbits that *Time* noted in its feature article on King was that he considered "loquacity . . . a vice." Boris Artzybasheff (1899–1965), 1942. Gouache on board, 27.3 x 24.1 cm (10¾ x 9½ in.). Syracuse University Art Collection, New York; gift of Mr. Boris Artzybasheff

moved when similar complaints reached him from officials within the government. A case in point was a letter he received from the head of the Office of War Information, Elmer Davis, in March 1943. In it, Davis took strenuous exception to the fact that King had seen fit to heavily edit an OWI story, intended for dissemination to newspapers, on the Joint Chiefs of Staff. In doing so, Davis charged, King had "stripped" the piece of "virtually all material which could make it of interest to the public" and thus had made it unpublishable.[10] No apology for this excessive blue-penciling was forthcoming, however. After scribbling a sarcastic "tut-tut!" in the margin, King relegated the letter to a file drawer, unanswered.

Interestingly enough, King's civilian boss, Frank Knox, was not immune to the admiral's imperiously tight-lipped policies. When an intermediary asked King why he chronically failed to keep Knox informed on various developments, King rejoined, "Why should I? The first thing he does is tell reporters everything he knows."[11]

But despite all this evidence of zealous concern for limiting the dispersal of news about naval activity, King did make one notable concession to the press. Beginning in late 1942, at first warily and then with some enthusiasm, he began holding regular confidential sessions with a small group of journalists, where he spoke relatively freely about America's current sea war. Acting on the advice of his lawyer, who feared that his closed mouth could engender enough criticism to jeopardize his position, King eventually realized that at least some members of the press could be trusted with his confidences. He also became aware that by sharing unpublishable information with these reporters, he was flattering them and, in the process, encouraging them to adopt a more sympathetic view toward his outlook on censorship. All in all, it was a tactic eminently worthy of a man who has been ranked among the most brilliant naval officers in American history.

## GENERAL DOUGLAS MACARTHUR
1880–1964

Admiral King's preference for stringent censorship policies grew out of a genuine anxiety that too free an airing of military information could heighten Axis effectiveness against the Allied cause. In the case of General Douglas MacArthur, who also was known to impose tight restrictions on the flow of wartime news, the source of motivation was quite another story.

Driven from the Philippines in the wake of the Japanese invasion of that strategically crucial archipelago, MacArthur had arrived in Australia in March 1942 to assume command of the Allies' Southwest Pacific operations. Shortly after doing so, he held a press conference, where he told reporters that they constituted "one of the most valuable components" in the struggle to subdue Japan, because "in democracies it is essential that the public know the truth."[12] Coming from MacArthur, whose impressive bearing and oracular speaking style seemed to give these words an unusually sincere weight, the reporters were understandably pleased. Not only did they have the good fortune to be stationed on an important front of the war; it also appeared that the man setting the policies on what they could and could not report subscribed to the notion that the franker and fuller the news coverage the better. As one reporter present on this occasion later put

it, "The correspondents were greatly heartened."[13]

In practice, however, MacArthur did not prove to be the enlightened godsend to their profession that the reporters initially perceived him to be. At the war's outset, he had a reputation as one of the most capable officers in the United States Army, and over the next four years, his many suc-

This portrait of MacArthur was painted in New Guinea. John C. Murphy (born 1919), 1944. Oil on canvas, 61.6 x 49.5 cm (24¼ x 19½ in.). Yale University Art Gallery, New Haven, Connecticut; gift of Mrs. Richard K. Sutherland

cessful drives against the Japanese, climaxing in the reoccupation of the Philippines, only reinforced the wisdom of that judgment. But MacArthur wanted more than to be remembered simply as one of the several great generals to come out of World War II; instead he was determined to be known as a general whose courage under fire and talent for delivering the decisive blow to his opponents at little cost in American lives were barely short of perfection. This ambition had significant implications for the journalists covering his Southwest Pacific theater. And what it all boiled down to was a basic rule of thumb tacitly set for reporters by MacArthur's press officers: if a news story did not sufficiently promote the general's reputation, it would have to be altered accordingly to pass through censorship.

Translated into practice, this principle expressed itself in a host of ways. For starters, reporters' opinion pieces that in any way reflected imperfectly on MacArthur were often barred from publication, and the press was actively discouraged from dwelling, in its homebound reports, on Allied casualties in MacArthur-directed actions, especially if their rate was high. The most-often-invoked words in that matter, among MacArthur's press officers, were "low" and "light." If a resourceful reporter had gained particulars about casualties that disputed those adjectives and made so bold as to include them in a story, the story simply did not pass.

At the same time, MacArthur was sometimes not pleased when field officers within his command received prominent coverage in the press. When, for example, General Robert Eichelberger found himself prominently featured in *Life* as a result of his success in forcing the Japanese out of key strongholds in New Guinea, he also found himself in hot water with MacArthur, who reminded this subordinate that it was in his power to have him demoted to colonel. As a result of this unwillingness to share the limelight with others, MacArthur's press office naturally did its best to keep news stories as sharply focused as possible on MacArthur as the architect of victory. The strategy for accomplishing that end could sometimes be subtle; for awhile in the summer of 1942, it took the form of an order to correspondents to insert MacArthur's name into their datelines, which now were to read "With General MacArthur's Headquarters."[14]

Considering this personalization of dateline unseemly, MacArthur's superiors in Washington quickly ordered the practice stopped. But there was another ploy for keeping the general's name in the forefront of news emanating from the Pacific, which continued largely unabated throughout the war—his press office's chronic habit of issuing communiqués to the press that focused almost exclusively on MacArthur as the instrument of Allied victory. When he was still in the Philippines, for example, in late 1941 and early 1942, leading the ill-fated battle to stave off the Japanese invasion, 109 out of the 142 communiqués issued by his press of-

Taken on Christmas Day 1942, this picture shows MacArthur standing on the grounds of Government House at Port Moresby in New Guinea. When the photograph was released to the press, however, its caption left the distinct impression that MacArthur was in some "tropic wilderness" combat area where he was personally leading the war against the Japanese. "A palpable fake picture, at least insofar as the caption is concerned," fumed journalist Lewis Sebring, who by then was heartily disgusted with the self-serving distortions coming from MacArthur's press office. Unidentified photographer, 1942. General Douglas MacArthur Memorial, Norfolk, Virginia

fice mentioned only MacArthur, creating the impression that he was fighting this heroic struggle alone.

But these efforts to bolster MacArthur's reputation seem minor and rather sophomoric compared to some others. The fact was that, in passing news of the Pacific war on to journalists, his press officers also routinely engaged in distortion. Thus, although two of the major Allied Pacific victories of 1942—the Battle of the Coral Sea and the prolonged struggle to drive the Japanese from Guadalcanal—took place in a theater under navy command, and although MacArthur was only tangentially involved in both, some of his communiqués conveyed the distinct impression that

he was in charge of both of them. MacArthur also habitually declared victory in his operations well before it could be claimed. On December 26, 1944, for example, some two months after his forces had begun retaking the Filipino island of Leyte, his press office pronounced in effect that Leyte was now secure, save for some "mopping up."[15] In reality, that mopping up took six months to complete against stiff enemy opposition and ultimately cost some seven hundred American lives.

In the matter of enemy losses, truth again often fell victim to a campaign to inflate MacArthur's reputation. Following the Battle of the Bismarck Sea in March 1943, a MacArthur communiqué announced that forces under his command had sunk 22 Japanese ships, downed 55 Japanese planes (a figure revised in a later communiqué to 102), and brought death to no fewer than 15,000 Japanese military personnel. The Bismarck Sea encounter was undoubtedly an American victory worth crowing about. But those stunningly impressive statistics were far from accurate. Subsequent investigations—corroborated later by documents in Japan's war archives—revealed that the enemy losses, though high, had been substantially less.

It is often said that photographs don't lie. In MacArthur's case, however, they sometimes did. For among his press office's abiding concerns was a desire to create the illusion that MacArthur was taking an active part in frontline action when he was not. The reasoning behind this was obvious: No matter how important MacArthur's work at his safe and secure headquarters might be, it was lacking in heroism. Consequently, his press office, on at least two occasions during the war, issued pictures with captions indicating that he was much closer to the line of battle than was actually the case. In one of those instances, the captions indicated that pictures showed MacArthur with troops in New Guinea as they were preparing to move up to the front lines there. But the pictures had really been taken at a training camp in Australia, far from any active combat. In the other instance, the MacArthur photograph in question was indeed taken in New Guinea. But the setting was not the island's enemy-infested jungle wilderness as its caption implied; rather it was the grounds of the subject's temporary headquarters, situated well away from the whizzing bullets of any hostile Japanese enclave.

For the reporters assigned to MacArthur's command, all of these public-relations exercises in aggrandizing one man contributed to a professional demoralization. Because a basic requirement for getting their stories through censorship in their theater was that their accounts had to square with press-office communiqués, they often felt that they were mere press agents, as indeed on many occasions they were. Moreover, when they made known their dissatisfaction with that role to MacArthur's press officers, they were in effect told to like it or lump it. In the face of that dictum, a number of them simply picked up and left. Those choosing to stay and adapt to the situation found solace by, among other things, passing around amusing poetic expressions of their unhappiness. One such self-mocking versification ran, in part: "Put on your spurs and pick up your whip; / Know ye the pleasures of censorship! / Take a deep drag on the juice of the poppy / And then cut the hell out of everyone's copy!"[16]

The most noteworthy fruit of these reporters' plight, however, was that MacArthur did indeed emerge from the war, in the eyes of many Americans, as a nearly flawless military genius. But in light of his genuinely good performance in the Pacific, that might have occurred without his press office's efforts to make it happen.

## ELMER DAVIS
### 1890–1958

In March 1942, with the country some three months into its struggle against the Axis powers, CBS radio news commentator Elmer Davis took out after the federal government's so-far-chaotic efforts to provide the American press and public with as true a picture of the war as the exigencies of military security would allow. Addressing this issue in his usual unmincing manner, this white-haired newsman, with a homespun Indiana twang that tended to make his words all the more credible, declared that "the whole government publicity situation has everybody in the news business almost in despair, with half a dozen agencies following different lines." But Davis had an alternative for this system of overlapping jurisdictions and its self-contradictory policies on just what war news was fit to print. The answer, he said, lay in the formation of a central agency "under one head" that would be empowered to set criteria for determining what news should be released and when, and to serve as the clearinghouse for its release. "Objection has been made," he continued, "that it might be hard to pick the man." Nevertheless, he added, "almost anybody would be better" than the "half a dozen heads" who were now charged with dispensing war information.[17]

Apparently President Franklin Roosevelt and his administration were coming to much the same conclusion as Davis. In

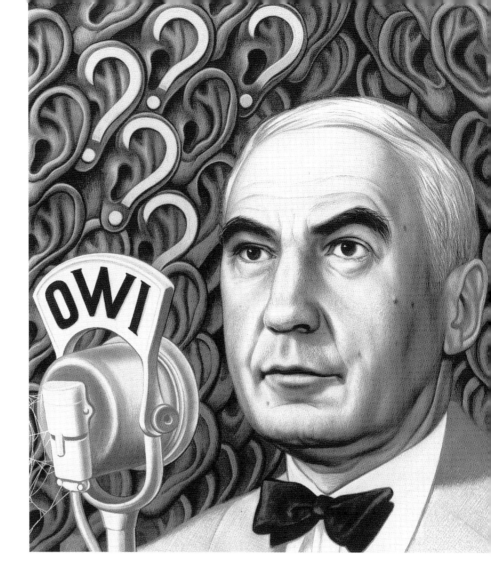

June 1942, Roosevelt created by executive order the Office of War Information, one of whose main purposes was indeed to serve as a clearinghouse for government war news and explanatory information on the country's war-related aims and policies. The individual, however, whom he chose to preside over this new organization was not the "almost anybody" that Davis claimed would do; rather it was Elmer Davis himself.

In accepting this appointment as the nation's information czar, Davis could see certain pitfalls that he earnestly wanted to avoid. Namely, he did not want his agency to become a mere propaganda machine in-

When this image of Elmer Davis appeared on the cover of *Time* in March 1943, Davis's Office of War Information was in trouble—accused, on the one hand, of being too propagandistic and, on the other, of being too frank in its approach to information dissemination. Boris Artzybasheff (1899–1965), 1943. Gouache on board, 27 x 23.8 cm (10⅝ x 9⅜ in.). Syracuse University Art Collection, New York; gift of Mr. Boris Artzybasheff

The Office of War Information's *Negroes and the War* was one of the ventures that got OWI into trouble with Congress and led to drastic cutbacks in its budget in mid-1943. Designed to inform the nation's African American community of what blacks were doing for the war effort, the publication adopted a much too positive view on the possibilities for greater racial equality in this country to suit the tastes of many influential southern congressmen. Suitland Reference Branch, National Archives, Suitland, Maryland

NEGROES and the WAR

tent on putting a roseate glow on the war news. "The American people and . . . all other peoples opposing the Axis aggressors" had a right, he said, "to be truthfully informed."[18] Although willing to acknowledge that military security might qualify that right on occasion, he was determined to provide the country with the "fullest and most accurate information possible." Such an approach seemed to most to be just what was needed, and the news that radio's reassuringly avuncular

"Mt. Everest of commentators" was to oversee OWI was greeted with widespread praise.[19]

Unfortunately, Davis's promise of candor was far easier to state than to achieve, and he and OWI were soon engulfed in a multitude of difficulties that drew criticism from many quarters. When it came to getting news out, for example, on current battlefront progress and weapons production, OWI found itself many times facing military authorities far less committed to full and honest news coverage than Davis. Amazingly enough, that barrier was sometimes thrown up even when the news was positive and had seemingly no chance of threatening the nation's wartime security. Thus, when OWI sought to circulate a government release announcing that United States warplane production had gone from 19,403 in 1941 to an impressively spirit-raising 47,694 in 1942, the Defense Department refused to clear the story on the rationale that airing this information would help the enemy much more than it would advance American civilian morale.

The consequence of all this was that Davis and OWI were continually facing charges in the press of backsliding on their initial promises. Heightening the credibility of those accusations were dissensions within OWI itself. These culminated in the spring of 1943 and focused on staff writers' claims that their colleagues were turning some of OWI's information-giving efforts into cheery morale-boosting sloganeering.

Ultimately Congress—particularly its anti-administration members—also became critical of OWI. Perhaps its greatest source of dissatisfaction was a perception that some of OWI's publications, designed for keeping the public informed on such matters as wartime taxation, were nothing more than partisan efforts to promote Roosevelt's popularity. Although grounds for imputing such a bias were tenuous at best, that did not stop many congressmen from characterizing Davis as a "propaganda minister for the New Deal," and America's answer to Hitler's chief public-relations man Joseph Goebbels.[20] Nor did it stop them from spearheading an ultimately successful drive, in June 1943, to substantially cut the funding for OWI's news-disseminating operations within the United States.

But despite all the criticism and funding cutbacks, Davis could look back at war's end on his tenure at OWI and count some notable successes in contributing to the truthfulness of the war's news coverage. Owing in large part to him, the government prohibition against publishing news photographs showing dead American soldiers was lifted in September 1943, so civilians at home were now allowed to confront in pictures one of the war's harshest realities, the loss of their own countrymen. Davis's pressuring also led to a more thorough press coverage of the Normandy invasion than the military would otherwise have permitted. More important than his victories on isolated matters such as these, however, was Davis's success in moving the military toward a view of the war's news coverage that was closer to his own. Although the army and navy never fully bought into his outlook on this matter, they had, thanks largely to OWI's prodding, by war's end appreciably liberalized their definition regarding what the public could or ought to be told.

## STANLEY JOHNSTON
### 1900–1962

*Chicago Tribune* reporter Stanley Johnston. Unidentified photographer, 1942. AP/ Wide World Photos

America's system of censorship during World War II generally imposed comparatively light penalties on newspapers and individual reporters found to be in violation of its rules. Because the press by and large honored the need for governmental controls over its news coverage, its breaches of censorship regulations were, more often than not, committed unconsciously. So, when they did occur, the chastisement most often called for amounted to little more than tactfully applied official wrist-slapping. In yet other instances, namely where a journalist seemed to have knowingly exceeded the bounds of a censorship mandate, the punishment could be more serious and could, for example, result in the suspension of a correspondent's credentials.

The government, however, had at its disposal a means for exacting a punishment for censorship violations that was far more stringent. It was called the Espionage Act, a law that dated from World War I and that made anyone communicating valuable information to an American enemy vulnerable to heavy fines or imprisonment or both. Those charged with administering the press-censorship policies of World War II were well aware of this tool for enforcing their rules, but they generally were loath to use it, feeling that, unless a violation was egregious, the matter should be settled in a more benign way. In fact, throughout the whole of the war, the government chose to invoke the Espionage Act against a member of the Fourth Estate only once.

The case in question focused on a report on the Battle of Midway that appeared in the *Chicago Tribune* on June 7, 1942, under a headline that read "Navy Had Word of Jap Plan to Strike at Sea."[21] The author of this account, Stanley Johnston, had not been present at this landmark American naval victory over the Japanese. Rather, having returned just a few days earlier to the *Tribune*'s Chicago headquarters from

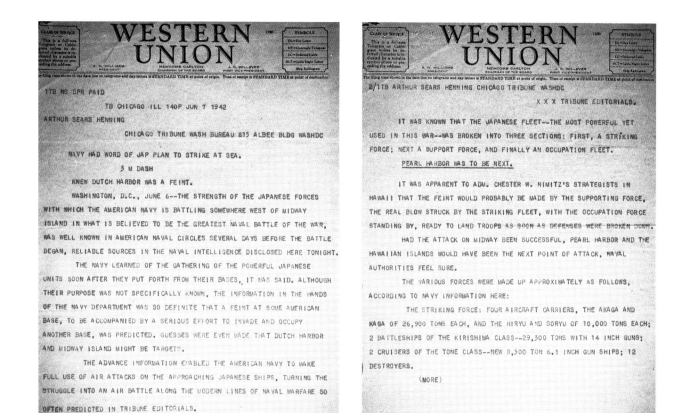

covering the Pacific war, he had pieced his Midway story together from official news communiqués about the battle and various bits of information to which he had been privy while in the Pacific. Chief among the latter was a secret dispatch from Admiral Chester Nimitz regarding the disposition and probable destination of Japanese ships on the eve of Midway, which Johnston had seen on his homeward voyage. The result was a story that, though composed several thousands of miles away from the actual event, was far more detailed and accurate than the security-minded navy would have liked, and its

publication left officials in Washington convulsed with a combination of panic and outrage. While efforts were soon afoot to prevent other newspapers from picking up Johnston's Midway account, members of the military establishment began demanding that Johnston and his editors at the *Tribune* be strung up from the highest tree.

The source of this anger was not so much the facts reported in the Johnston article per se. It was, instead, what the precision of those facts, in combination with the story's declaration of the navy's foreknowledge of the Japanese attack at Mid-

Part of the cable version of Johnston's Midway story, with its false Washington, D.C., dateline. Civil Reference Branch, National Archives, Washington, D.C.

way, stood to reveal about the American military's ability to penetrate Japan's most secret wartime codes. The Nimitz dispatch on the composition and intentions of a Midway-bound Japanese armada had been the invaluable fruit of the navy's success in breaking those codes. And now, thanks to Johnston, Washington's wartime strategists feared that the Japanese would soon be deducing that it was time to make drastic alterations in their radio communications codes. In other words, there was a strong possibility that the Allies' most valuable source of information on the strengths, weaknesses, and future war

plans of their Pacific opposition was about to be lost until the replacement codes could be penetrated. In light of that disastrous prospect, Johnston's Midway story thus unquestionably represented a breach of national security that demanded a strong redress. By late July 1942, the government was preparing to prosecute the reporter and the *Chicago Tribune* on charges of violating the Espionage Act.

Although the decision to prosecute was based mostly on the real and substantial damage that the Midway story could do to the Allied cause, another factor was also involved. The proprietor of the *Chicago Tribune* was Colonel Robert McCormick, whose rabid hatred for President Roosevelt had made the *Tribune* a vocal and often troublesome critic of Roosevelt's administration. Consequently, doubtless more than a few officials in wartime Washington saw this as a golden opportunity for evening the score against McCormick.

Whatever the motivation, the attempt to bring Johnston and the *Tribune* to justice failed, but not for want of evidence. Rather, the government was reluctant to reveal that evidence in its entirety to the grand jury that assembled in Chicago in early August for purposes of indicting Johnston and his newspaper. Thus, while the prosecution aggressively and convincingly pressed its point that Johnston had without proper naval authorization based his Midway story largely on Admiral Nimitz's dispatch, it withheld the fact that Johnston's story had seriously risked re-

An army photograph of a Japanese ship heavily damaged at the Battle of Midway. Unidentified photographer, 1942. Still Picture Branch, National Archives, Washington, D.C.

vealing to the Japanese that their opponent had broken their codes.

The reason for not mentioning that vital detail, which might well have damned Johnston in the grand jury's eyes as the greatest traitor since Benedict Arnold, was not difficult to understand: After all, there was still a good chance that the Japanese had not caught on to the implicit indication that their coded messages were being read. If, however, the prosecution explicitly revealed this deepest of Allied military secrets in this court proceeding, which was being widely covered by the press, that chance would disappear altogether, and the probability that the Japanese would alter their codes accordingly would become a dead certainty. But however sound the rationale for this inhibited strategy was, the prosecution's unwillingness to disclose the full nature of the government's grievance against Johnston made for a decidedly weak argument for indictment. Ultimately, the grand jury declared that Johnston's alleged offenses against the nation's military security were not justifiable grounds for trying him and the *Tribune* under the Espionage Act.

The tale of Johnston's journalistic indiscretions was not over. Immediately following the airing of his Midway story on June 7, the Japanese apparently had not picked up on the article's implications regarding the Allied breaking of their codes, and through the rest of June and July the codes went unchanged. Circumstantial evidence indicates that the widely published reports of the Johnston-*Tribune* grand jury

trial in early August, however, did alert them to the possibility that their ciphers had been compromised. Within a week of Johnston's court hearings, the American army and navy's worst fears became a reality: The Japanese altered their military codes, and it was many months before the revised ciphers were finally broken.

One of the most intriguing aspects of this incident remains an enigma even today. Surely it crossed the minds of both Johnston and his *Tribune* editors that the Midway account gave away an important intelligence secret. After all, if the navy knew "in advance" about the movement of Japanese ships, it followed almost automatically that it had tapped into the enemy's secret communication system. Moreover, there is evidence—namely a false Washington, D.C., dateline—indicating that the *Tribune* sensed this to be the case and that to avoid chastisement it had tried to make it look as if the story came from an authorized government source. So the question arises: Why did the *Tribune* run Johnston's story without first deleting its security-breaching facts and phraseology? Was it a conscious lack of patriotism? Could it have been meant as a way for the paper to thumb its nose at the wartime administration of its longtime adversary Franklin Roosevelt? Or was it simply a case of zeal for an exclusive heedlessly carried too far? The last conjecture is probably closest to the truth. But since no one at the *Tribune* ever satisfactorily explained the paper's behavior, the answer will always remain murky.

# 3

# PUTTING THE WAR IN FOCUS

## THE PHOTOGRAPHERS

Of all the branches of the journalistic profession, none played a more central role in reporting the events of World War II to the American public than photography. The photographs from that conflict number into the millions; to tabulate their total any more precisely would require a herculean effort. But the sheer massiveness of the camera record is not its only noteworthy aspect. Equally important is the fact that the news photographers' archive of World War II contains some of the most memorable examples of reportage to come out of that conflict, and for a good many Americans, photography was the main journalistic vehicle for learning about World War II.

In contrast with previous wars, the prominence of news photography as a purveyor of information during World War II constituted a great sea change. Generally speaking, the photographic coverage of earlier wars had been relatively limited and, in the business of reporting frontline action, had played a role that was decidedly inferior to the written word. To a great extent, the state of photographic technology simply could not provide news photographers with the ability to produce pictures capable of holding their own against printed accounts of war. During World War I, for example, the cameras available to frontline photographers possessed only limited capabilities for capturing the quick movement and momentary randomness of battle. As a result, even the best of the news photographs from that bloody four-year conflict generally depicted the static, undramatic prologues and aftermaths of frontline actions rather than their heart. Technological advances in the 1920s and 1930s, however, changed all that. With the development of more compact and portable cameras, faster films, more powerful lenses, and vastly accelerated shutter speeds, the camera's potential for chronicling the drama of war was greatly enhanced.

But the camera's increased adaptability to wartime conditions was not the only factor that contributed to its prominent part in the story of the journalistic coverage of World War II. Also important was the development, following World War I, of the capacity to transmit photographs over long distances—even oceans—via radio, telegraph, and telephone, which meant that pictures taken on some distant continent could now reach the editorial offices of newspapers and magazines within hours, if not minutes, of their being shot. Thus, the visual reportage of distant news events was no longer subject to lengthy delays in transmission that in the past had frequently made it passé by the time it reached its point of publication.

Adding yet further to photography's importance as a news conveyer in the years just before World War II was an increasing interest within journalism in expanding its uses. Armed with better cameras, photographers were getting better pictures, and this, combined with improved techniques for printing them, inevitably heightened their effect on the printed page. That in turn led to the advent of the photo essay, which attempted to serve up the news as much as possible through pictures rather than words. Originating in European publications, the photo essay began taking strong hold in American journalism in the mid-1930s with the establishment of *Life,* a magazine that from the outset gave the picture story preeminence. *Life*'s visual approach to the news proved a huge success from the moment it first hit the newsstands, and as its circulation soared, other publications started in varying degrees to imitate it.

In other words, by the eve of World War II, photojournalism had come into its own. It was now recognized as an entity onto itself, with its own dignity and special capabilities for vividly reporting the news of the world. So as Japan and Germany launched their drives for hegemony in Asia and Europe in the late 1930s, America's professional news photographers were well poised for the task of creating the most informative visual chronicle of war that had yet been made.

## MARGARET BOURKE-WHITE

1904–1971

Among those best poised for this task was *Life* photographer Margaret Bourke-White. In her youth Bourke-White had harbored ambitions for a career in biology. But in college she took up photography more or less as a sideline, and during her final undergraduate years at Cornell University, armed with a secondhand camera, she helped to defray her tuition expenses by taking and selling pictures of Cornell's campus. In the process, she found that she had both a flair and a passion for such work. By the time she received her A.B. degree in 1927, she was determined to make her way as a professional photographer. Within a few more years, she was thriving as a freelancer, with a studio headquarters in New York City's Chrysler Building, and was fast building a reputation as one of the best industrial and architectural photographers around.

In 1935 Bourke-White joined the staff of *Life* while it was still in its formative stages. When the magazine finally made its appearance late the following year, her picture essay on the construction of a New Deal dam in Montana was the main story. As other photo stories by her appeared in *Life* over the next several years, Bourke-White's stature grew, and by the late 1930s she stood at the top of her profession. Commenting on her series for *Life* depicting the daily rhythms of the residents of Muncie, Indiana, for example, America's leading arbiter of contemporary photography, Beaumont Newhall, had declared it "the finest piece of documentary photography" that he had ever seen.[1]

Bourke-White's first direct encounter with World War II came in the late spring and early summer of 1941. *Life* editor Wilson Hicks had a feeling that the mutual nonaggression pact, which the Soviet Union had signed with Germany a few weeks before the outbreak of war in Europe back in 1939, was about to come apart. In all likelihood, the dissolution of that agreement would mark the beginning of a Nazi invasion of Soviet territory, and if his hunch was correct, he was anxious that one of his photo correspondents should be in the Soviet Union once the shooting started. His choice for this assignment was Bourke-White, and after a roundabout journey across the Pacific and through Asia, she and her then-husband, writer Erskine Caldwell, arrived in Moscow in early May. So thanks to Hicks's prescience, Bourke-White found herself, some seven weeks later, with a scoop of the first magnitude on her hands. On June 22, 1941, Hitler's armies began rolling across the Soviet Union's European border, and as the only foreign photojournalist then in the Soviet Union, she had the chance for an exclusive story that most members of the press could only dream about.

Or so it seemed. For although Bourke-White was definitely at the right place at the right time, there was one hurdle that she had to leap before she could set to

work: The Soviet military authorities had issued an edict that anyone found taking pictures of the invasion would be shot on sight. As a result, it appeared that if she chose to remain in the Soviet Union against the kindly advice of the American ambassador, she would end up cooling her heels in her luxurious, cherub-bedecked Moscow hotel room overlooking the Kremlin.

One of Bourke-White's greatest virtues as a photographer, however, was a single-minded determination to get what she wanted. That trait on occasion caused her trouble, and when, later in the war, she wanted to go to the Italian front, her reputation for wanting to shoot the war on her own terms and in defiance of military-correspondent regulations resulted in some troublesome delays in her obtaining permission to go there. But in the Soviet Union, her determination put her in good stead. After weeks of pleading via an unremitting stream of letters, phone calls, and personal interviews, she won permission on July 15 to go to work.

The permission came none too soon. Four days later, German bombers launched their first night attack on Moscow, and when the Luftwaffe returned the following evening for another raid, Bourke-White, with her cameras stationed on the roof of the American embassy, was there to record it. Before she left the Soviet Union, Bourke-White would have many other opportunities to photograph air attacks on the Soviet capital from her hotel balcony and in the process obtain

many remarkable shots of the Kremlin dramatically silhouetted against a sky lit by ground fires from below and Nazi flares from above. But this first experience with recording a night air raid on the roof of the American embassy, she later recalled, would always remain one of the outstanding memories of her career.

Initiation into the art of photographing German air attacks was not the only vivid memory that Bourke-White took away with her when she finally returned to the United States late in September. Although permission to use her camera did not initially include permission to witness the Soviet-German land war, her continued wheedling eventually got her close enough to the actual lines of battle to record some of the devastations visited on Soviet civilians. More memorable yet was her success in winning a picture-taking audience with the Soviet Union's wartime leader, Joseph Stalin—an opportunity that had never before been accorded to an American photographer.

Margaret Bourke-White surrounded by Russian soldiers during her stay in the Soviet Union in the late spring and summer of 1941. Unidentified photographer. Margaret Bourke-White Papers, Special Collections Department, Syracuse University Library, New York. © Time Warner Inc.

Aerial camera used by Margaret Bourke-White during the war. Margaret Bourke-White Papers, Special Collections Department, Syracuse University Library, New York

Bourke-White shot this scene of a German air raid over Moscow from her hotel room's balcony overlooking the Kremlin. During air raids Bourke-White was expected, like all Muscovites, to retreat to a shelter. She had other ideas, however, and on a number of occasions when wardens checked her room to see that she had gone to a shelter, she had to desert her picture-making endeavors to hide under her bed. Margaret Bourke-White for *Life* magazine, 1941. © Time Warner Inc.

At the time of Germany's surrender in May 1945, some German civilians, unable to face defeat and military occupation, committed suicide. Bourke-White happened upon one such instance at Leipzig's city hall, where a number of local officials—some with their families—had retreated to their wood-paneled offices and swallowed cyanide. Reproduced here is her shot of the dead wife and daughter of Leipzig's assistant mayor. Margaret Bourke-White for *Life* magazine, 1945. © Time Warner Inc.

When Bourke-White encountered Soviet dictator Joseph Stalin in his Kremlin office, she was struck by his shortness, and her first thought was: "What an insignificant-looking man!" As she prepared to photograph him, however, her perception changed. "I decided," she later wrote, "there was nothing insignificant about Stalin. Many correspondents . . . wondered whether Stalin made his own decisions or was merely a figurehead. One look at that granite face, and I was sure Stalin made all the decisions." Margaret Bourke-White for *Life* magazine, 1941. © Time Warner Inc.

Bourke-White's success in getting what she wanted from Soviet officials testified to her considerable skills in persuasion. But apparently they had their limits when it came to trying to make Stalin smile. Reminiscing about the stubbornly sober Soviet dictator, she once noted that he "was one of the few subjects . . . who would not obey me."[2] However, what Bourke-White's charm and cajoling could not do, the accidental spilling of her flashbulbs did. While she hastily stooped to retrieve the bulbs as they bounced across the floor, Stalin's face betrayed amusement that lasted just long enough for Bourke-White to take a picture showing the faint but unmistakable traces of the sought-after grin.

As a woman, Bourke-White often came up against a strong reluctance on the part of the military to grant her the same latitude accorded male correspondents in the matter of going into hazardous combat situations. On one noteworthy occasion, that reluctance worked to her advantage. In late 1942, she was preparing to go to North Africa to cover Allied operations there, when word came that, unlike a number of male journalists headed in the same direction, she would not be allowed to travel by plane because it was deemed too dangerous for a woman. Instead, she had to go by boat, which presumably was much safer. On the subsequent voyage, however, the ship she was on encountered a German U-boat torpedo and eventually

sank. A positive result of this otherwise unfortunate incident was another Bourke-White scoop—a lengthy photo story on the life-threatening hazards of wartime sea travel.

Eventually Bourke-White became quite adept at overcoming the army's hesitancy to let her venture into perilous situations. Within a few weeks of arriving in North Africa, after repeated denials of her requests for permission to accompany an air bombing mission, she finally found someone in authority who would say yes. On January 22, 1943, her aerial camera firmly in hand, she became the first woman to fly on an American combat mission, and by war's end, she had managed to see and record enough frontline action to satisfy any war correspondent—male or female.

While covering World War II, Bourke-White photographed many instances of the tragic human devastation that the conflict had wrought. Among her most moving wartime pictures were those depicting the heaped corpses and the grotesquely emaciated "living dead" that the Allies found when they entered the German concentration camps in the spring of 1945. After taking such pictures, Bourke-White wondered more than once how she had managed to keep her camera going in the face of the enormous suffering around her. The answer, she found, lay in a psychic mechanism born of professional necessity, which seemed automatically to click in as the occasion demanded. Remembering the shots she had made in Russia of the huddled bodies of a dead family killed in a

German air raid, Bourke-White wrote of this phenomenon: *It is a peculiar thing about pictures of this sort. It is as though a protecting screen draws itself across my mind and makes it possible to consider focus and light values and the technique of photography, in as impersonal a way as though I were making an abstract camera composition. This blind lasts as long as it is needed—while I am actually operating the camera. Days later, when I developed the negatives, I was surprised to find that I could not bring myself to look at the films.*[3]

## ROBERT CAPA
1913–1954

In 1936, a young Hungarian émigré named André Friedman was working as a news photographer in Paris. In his early twenties, he was beginning to do pretty well for himself as a freelancer. But he was anxious to do better, and after giving the problem some thought, he came up with a scheme that involved posing as the darkroom assistant of a famed but purely fictitious American photographer named Robert Capa and selling his own pictures to the press under the allegedly brilliant American's name. With his girlfriend serving as Capa's agent, the plot worked like a charm. Soon Friedman's work was selling at a substantially healthier clip and for higher fees as well. Moreover, Friedman became thoroughly enamored with the glamorous and internationally acclaimed figment of his imagination, and when an editor caught on to his deception, rather than letting Capa die, he decided it was time to make Capa a reality. From that moment on, André Friedman was Robert Capa.

The new flesh-and-blood Capa quickly measured up to his fabricated billing. By the summer of 1936, he was in Spain photographing the civil war there between the loyalist Republicans and the reactionary fascist right. It was here that he discovered the branch of photography that would make him even more celebrated than his fictional counterpart might ever have

dreamed of becoming. For, in turning his camera on this struggle, Capa found he had a special knack for capturing military action, and he was soon turning out a series of pictures that, for the first time in the history of photography, seemed to depict war in all its momentary and tragic immediacy. The most persuasive evidence of his ability was the picture he took in September 1936 that has come to be known simply as the "Falling Soldier." It showed a Spanish loyalist on a hillside, his arms outstretched and his back arched in agony from the impact of a fatally directed enemy bullet. Here, as never before, was a photographic distillation of what armed warfare was.

This photograph of Robert Capa was taken just before he set off on a paratroop drop into Germany in March 1945. When all was set for him to go, two cameras were tied to his legs, and a flask of scotch was in his breast pocket. "Fifteen minutes before I had to jump," Capa later quipped, "I started thinking over my life. I went over everything I ever ate and did and I finished up in twelve minutes." Unidentified photographer, 1945. © 1945, 1993 Robert Capa Archive, International Center of Photography, New York City

Several years later, writing about his work as a recorder of war, Capa wrote: "Slowly I am feeling more and more like a hyena. Even if you know the value of your works, it gets on your nerves. Everybody suspects that you . . . want to make money at the expense of other people's skins."[4] Such ruminations notwithstanding, Capa's reputation as an uncommonly adroit photographer of armed conflict sharply escalated in the next several years. By late 1938, following the publication of his pictures in *Life* and elsewhere of China's struggle to stave off its Japanese invaders, he was being hailed in both European and American press circles as "The Greatest War-Photographer in the World."[5]

Given his credentials, it would seem natural that, once World War II broke out, Capa should have been there in the thick of it recording its course practically from the outset. Instead, a combination of circumstances kept him at the war's periphery in its initial stages, and his early war-related photo stories for various publications were focused on such things as the effects of German air bombing on Great Britain.

Not the least of Capa's problems in getting close to the war was his national origin. Although he had transferred his base of operation to New York City in 1939, he nevertheless remained technically a citizen of Hungary, which by late 1940 had entered the Axis fold. As a result, when the United States finally declared war on the Axis powers following Pearl Harbor, Capa found himself categorized as an en-

emy alien. In January 1942, he received a letter from the federal government informing him that in the name of national security he had to turn in his cameras and that he was now forbidden to travel more than ten miles from New York.

With some wire-pulling, the bans against travel within the United States and against the use of his cameras were lifted within a relatively short time. But getting to any of the war's battlefronts was another matter. Although a bit more wire-pulling at the British embassy in Washington resulted in some irregularly improvised travel papers that enabled him to go to England as a correspondent for *Collier's,* the United States Army correspondent accreditation that would permit him to travel to the front lines of Allied military activity proved frustratingly elusive. It was not until March 1943 that the "Greatest War-Photographer in the World" was finally on his way to cover the final stages of the Allied drive to push the Germans from North Africa.

Late starter though he was, Capa ultimately produced some memorable pictures of the war. Transferring from *Collier's* to *Life* shortly before joining the Allied invasion of Sicily in mid-1943, he was on hand to record newsworthy military actions in the Italian campaign, the invasion of France, and the last days of fighting in Germany.

Of photographing combat, Capa once said that "if your pictures aren't good enough, you aren't close enough."[6] Capa lived by those words in pursuing his war-

This picture from the landing at Normandy may be the one that Capa was thinking of when he wrote in his memoir: "The men from my barge waded in the water. . . . I paused for a moment on the gangplank to take my first real picture of the invasion. The boatswain who was in a hurry to get the hell out of there, mistook my picture-taking attitude for explicable hesitation, and helped me make up my mind with a well-aimed kick in the rear." Robert Capa for *Life* magazine, 1944. Magnum Photos, Inc. © 1944, 1993 Robert Capa/Magnum Photos

Upon reaching the Normandy beach where he shot this picture of soldiers plodding through the water from their landing crafts in the distance, the first thing Capa did was throw himself flat on the sand to escape German fire. In that position he found himself "nose to nose" with a lieutenant. "He asked me if I knew what he saw," Capa recalled. "I told him . . . that I didn't think he could see much beyond my head." To which his prostrate companion answered, "I see my ma . . . waving my insurance policy." Robert Capa for *Life* magazine, 1944. Magnum Photos, Inc. © 1944, 1993 Robert Capa/Magnum Photos

Capa later said that for him the liberation of Paris in August 1944 "was the most unforgettable day in the world." But the Allied arrival in the city was not all jubilation. In Capa's photograph here, Parisians huddle on the pavement outside the Hôtel de Ville as shots from collaborationist snipers ring out in the area. Robert Capa for *Life* magazine, 1944. Magnum Photos, Inc. © 1944, 1993 Robert Capa/Magnum Photos

time assignments, going, for example, on the first invasion wave into Normandy and joining a paratroop drop behind enemy lines in Germany. Understandably there were times when being in the front lines as an unarmed observer became a duty that he would much rather have avoided. But to a large extent Capa had only himself to blame for some of the perils he faced in World War II, for one of his more noteworthy traits was an earthy and insouciant affability that quickly ingratiated him to soldiers and frequently led to invitations to accompany them on hazardous

missions. "I'm getting too popular," he once remarked of this phenomenon, "and someday this popularity will get me killed."[7]

Among Capa's most significant assignments during World War II was his coverage of the Allied Normandy invasion. Professionally it was also his most heartbreaking. One of only four news photographers allowed to accompany this most momentous operation on its first day, June 6, 1944, he characteristically later passed off the experience rather casually. After making his way ashore from a landing craft under heavy fire from well-fortified German guns stationed above the beach, he told a friend that he had found himself in an "unpleasant" spot, but "having nothing else to do, I started shooting pictures."[8]

In all, Capa managed to shoot some seventy-odd frames of the battle for Normandy in its first hours when the Allied forces' capacity to secure a foothold on the French coast remained questionable. With German guns "enjoying open season" on the vulnerable mass of armed humanity swarming ashore, a good many of those photographs were taken from a prone position—or, as Capa later put it, from "the sardine's angle," and after several hours of focusing and refocusing his camera on the bloody chaos, Capa had had enough of these adverse conditions.[9] Having run out of film, he beat a retreat to the ship that had brought him across the English Channel, its decks now littered with wounded.

Despite the relative shortness of his stay at Normandy, Capa came away with what he had gone there for, and then some. When *Life* staffers in London began developing his negatives, the prediction was that his pictures would prove to be unassailably the best from the invasion. Unfortunately this triumphant euphoria was short-lived. Amid *Life*'s haste to process Capa's work so that it would reach New York in time for the magazine's next issue, someone put the negatives into a drying cabinet and set it on high. There the films' emulsion began to melt, and by the time

VICTORIOUS YANK

MAY 14, 1945 10 CENTS

this darkroom mistake was caught, only eleven images, most of them slightly blurred from the heat, remained publishable. In his written recollections of Normandy, Capa himself never alluded to the fierce disappointment he must have felt on hearing of this disaster. As for *Life*, it chose to attribute the fuzziness of his pictures to the "immense excitement" that Capa had experienced in taking them.[10]

Capa spent the last weeks of the war in

Capa's photograph of Corporal Strickland as it appeared on the cover of *Life* marking the end of the war in Europe. Robert Capa for *Life* magazine, May 15, 1945. © Time Warner Inc.

Europe witnessing the final death throes of Nazi Germany. As the imminence of German surrender became ever more certain, *Life* asked him and its other photographers in Europe to produce a picture that would be appropriate for the cover of its issue marking that event, whenever it came. It is not known whether Capa had this request in mind when he rode into Nuremburg in April 1945 and met up with Corporal Hubert Strickland, who had been his jeep driver at the liberation of Paris the previous summer. In any case, the fortuitous reunion of the photographer and his driver yielded precisely the pictorial epitaph on the war in Europe that *Life* was looking for. On the cover of its first issue following the German surrender on May 7, 1945, the magazine featured Capa's picture of Strickland, standing before the huge swastika at Nuremburg's sports stadium and jubilantly offering a mock Nazi salute. Another Capa picture in the same issue, however, sounded a decidedly more somber note. Taken shortly before the one at Nuremburg, it showed an American soldier lying dead in his own blood on an apartment balcony in Leipzig, the victim of a German sniper.

With those two sharply contrasting photographs, Capa's role as a chronicler of World War II came to an end. He now began to toy with having cards printed up that read: "ROBERT CAPA/War Photographer/Unemployed."[11]

Capa's photograph of a fallen American soldier in Leipzig was among the last pictures he took of the war. Later Capa was present when the German snipers who had killed the soldier were forced to surrender. Robert Capa for *Life* magazine, 1945. Magnum Photos, Inc. © 1945, 1993 Robert Capa/Magnum Photos

Carl Mydans in Manila in 1945. Unidentified photographer for *Life* magazine. © Time Warner Inc.

## CARL MYDANS
BORN 1907

World War II was a conflict that left few parts of the globe unaffected. As a result, a good many correspondents charged with covering that conflict found themselves literally circling the globe as the reporting needs of their publications demanded. Among the war's more peripatetic journalists, few were more wide-ranging than *Life* photographer Carl Mydans. Although he may not have held the record for miles traveled in search of his war stories, it was certainly not for want of trying.

Having joined *Life*'s staff in 1936, Mydans was in New York when Hitler launched his invasion of Poland in September 1939. Within two weeks he was on his way to Europe, where his first assignment was to cover Great Britain's wartime preparations. But no sooner had he settled into that task than the Russian army began its invasion of Finland. By January 1940, dressed for subzero weather and his cameras tucked carefully under his thick outer jacket to prevent their freezing up, he was braving Finland's arctic winter to record the Finnish army's valiant but doomed effort to drive off its would-be conquerors. From there he went to Italy, where despite continual harassment from fascist Blackshirts, he managed among other things to focus his lens on Hitler's chief ally, Mussolini, as the Italian dictator, to paraphrase *Life,* "strutted his stuff" at public ceremonies in Rome. And in June 1940, when the

German Wehrmacht plowed across the allegedly impregnable French Maginot Line as if it were made of Tinkertoys, he was on hand to witness the fall of France. Then it was on to China to report the progress of Japan's invasion there. By the fall of 1941, he and his wife Shelley, a writer for *Life* who often worked with him, were in the Philippines assigned to stories on its defense preparations against the possibility of being overrun by Japan.

By then Mydans had traveled some 45,000 miles in the pursuit of his picture stories. But there were still many more miles to go. In 1944, he was with Allied forces in Italy when they entered Rome, and by summer of that year he was covering American military operations in southern France. And then it was back to the war in the Pacific, where early in 1945 he ultimately turned his cameras on the American reconquest of the Philippines. Finally, on September 2, 1945, he was on board the United States battleship *Missouri,* anchored in a Japanese harbor, photographing Japan's signing of an unconditional surrender to the Allies.

In scanning this diverse itinerary, it is not hard to discern a long gap during which Mydans seems to have dropped out of the business of covering the war. Indeed, that is exactly what happened, but it was not the result of personal choice. For when Carl and Shelley Mydans arrived in the Philippines in October 1941, they were unknowingly headed into a situation that would soon transform them from detached observers of the world's

When *Life* assigned Mydans to Italy in 1940, he found himself routinely shadowed by fascist Blackshirts who had apparently been ordered to thwart his picture-taking as much as possible. Despite harassment from the Blackshirts, Mydans managed to catch this shot of Mussolini (*center*) looking every inch the arrogant dictator at public ceremonies in Rome. *Life* published the picture over a caption that identified Mussolini as "the elderly butcher boy of fascism." This insolence resulted in the expulsion of the magazine's entire Italian staff from Italy. Carl Mydans for *Life* magazine, 1940. © Time Warner Inc.

events—relatively free to come and go as they wished—to entrapped participants. The beginning of that change in status occurred December 8, 1941, when following their surprise attack on Pearl Harbor the previous day, the Japanese launched their invasion of the Philippines.

For awhile Mydans reacted to this turn of events much as he had to other newsworthy occurrences in the past: he turned his camera on them. But as Japanese bombs battered the Filipino capital of Manila and virtually wiped out the contingent of warplanes at the nearby American airfield, and as Japanese ground forces moved toward Manila from the north, tak-

ing pictures became a decidedly less important concern. As Christmas drew near, it was clear to Mydans and his wife that the chief business at hand was finding a means of escape from this country before the Japanese had fully occupied it. Unfortunately, however, every time the Mydanses thought they had lined up a place on a ship that could spirit them away, the vessel in question was sunk or turned away. As a result, shortly after the Japanese army marched into Manila on January 2, 1942, Carl and Shelley Mydans found themselves—along with hundreds of other stranded American civilians—prisoners of war. Shortly before that, *Life*, clearly ig-

The armband that Mydans was compelled to wear during his imprisonment in Shanghai by the Japanese. Private collection

The men pictured in this photograph, taken by Mydans in February 1945, had been in the Santo Tomás prison camp for more than three years and during Mydans's incarceration there had been two of his roommates. While at Santo Tomás, they had lost 131 pounds between them. Carl Mydans for *Life* magazine, 1945. © Time Warner Inc.

norant of the rapid deterioration of Filipino defenses, had wired the couple asking for some positive reports of success in
keeping the encroaching Japanese at bay,
and Shelley Mydans had cabled back,
"Bitterly regret your request unavailable
here."[12] When she made that gloomy as-
sessment, she sensed its unhappy implications for herself and her husband, but
when those implications became a reality,
having recognized them beforehand did
not make them any easier to bear.

In all, the Mydanses' imprisonment
lasted some twenty-one months. The first
site of their incarceration was sexually
segregated facilities in buildings of the
University of Santo Tomás on the outskirts
of Manila, where at the outset the prisoners were largely left to their own devices
in fending for food and organizing their
routines. The situation was not altogether
impossible, and before long there was an
improvised system of medical care and
prisoner self-government. Still, there were
hardships and privations. During the first
few days of living thirty to a room and
scavenging sustenance from sympathetic
Filipino natives who were allowed to pass
food to the prisoners through the com-
pound's fences, Mydans found himself recalling the observation of a man he once
met who had been a prisoner during World
War I. As an enemy captive, he told Mydans, "first you are worried that you will
be killed. Then, when you are not killed,
you think, 'Well at least I can sit.' And
then you find that it is not the way you like
to sit."[13]

After eight months at Santo Tomás,
Carl and Shelley Mydans became the ben-
eficiaries of a misunderstanding in the
Japanese prison hierarchy. Pursuant to an
order that was not originally meant to
apply to them, they and about 125 fellow
inmates were transferred to Shanghai,
where initially they were allowed a limited freedom and then once again herded
into a crowded camp. Ultimately this
change of location won them their liberation. In the fall of 1943 they became part
of a prisoner exchange, and they were
back in New York City in time for
Christmas.

Mydans lost no time in resuming his
tasks as a wartime chronicler, and once
his correspondent's accreditation came
through from the army in the spring of
1944, he was back to his roaming ways.
Covering the remainder of the war in both
Europe and the Pacific, he produced many
distinguished news pictures, not least of
which were a shot of a French collaborator
being executed and one of General Douglas MacArthur wading ashore at Luzon in
the Philippines early in 1945.

But by far the most personally satis-
fying event in the final chapter of Mydans's wartime wanderings occurred on
February 3, 1945. Attached that day to an
American army force of some seven hundred men that was wending its perilous
way out of Manila through still-strong
pockets of Japanese resistance, he found
himself, as evening descended, approaching the gates of Santo Tomás. As he
set eyes on this place of his captivity

When General Douglas MacArthur's Pacific forces landed at Luzon in the Philippines early in 1945, Mydans had the good fortune to be on MacArthur's ship, and so he became the photographer to make this picture of MacArthur coming triumphantly ashore. The image's sense of heroic intrepidness, however, was as much MacArthur's doing as it was Mydans's. For it was MacArthur who, unbeknownst to Mydans stationed on shore, had decided to wade onto Luzon rather than to have his landing craft drop him off on the beach. Years later Mydans said of MacArthur: "No one I have ever known . . . had a better understanding of the drama and power of a picture." Carl Mydans for *Life* magazine, 1945. © Time Warner Inc.

again, he felt ill. The nausea, however, was only momentary, and he was soon in the vanguard moving behind two army tanks toward one of the buildings that still housed his fellow inmates. Inside it was silent and dark save for a few flickering candles. But after the building's residents realized that their night visitors were liberating Americans and not a contingent of Japanese guards, the atmosphere became one of joyous pandemonium, made all the more joyous when it became known that one of the prison's liberators was also a former inhabitant. "Carl Mydans. My God! It's Carl Mydans," cried a female inmate as the bearer of that name directed a flashlight across his own face.[14] With that, the other prisoners suddenly engulfed him, amiably shoved him onto a staircase, and called for a speech. The speech did not amount to much. Nevertheless, it was the moment that counted, and measured against it, even the privilege of shooting pictures of the official Japanese surrender on the *Missouri* seven months later was something of an anticlimax.

## LEE MILLER
1907–1977

Given its longstanding reputation for ex-
quisite picture spreads of soigné models
swathed in expensive silks and furs and
slick advertisements for perfume, hats,
and kid gloves, *Vogue* was hardly the sort
of publication where one would expect to
find reportage on the harsh realities of
World War II. And by and large, that was
the case. Aside from such articles as "How
Couturiers Are Coping with War Conditions" and "What People Are Wearing in
Air-Raid Shelters," the issues of *Vogue* between 1939 and 1945 did not let global
war impinge a great deal on its preoccupation with reporting the latest trends of
high fashion.

In this picture, taken in northern France in 1944, Lee
Miller wears a helmet, of her
own design, with a movable
front that would enable her to
take pictures while still wearing it. Unidentified photographer, 1944. © Lee Miller Archives, 1993

*Top right:*
Miller titled this photograph
of bombed-out statuary in
London *Revenge on Culture.*
Published in *Grim Glory,* it
was one of that book's most
widely praised pictures. Lee
Miller, circa 1941. © Lee
Miller Archives, 1993

*Bottom right:*
This picture of an army field
hospital in France was taken
by Lee Miller during her first
assignment as an official war
correspondent for *Vogue.* Lee
Miller, 1944. © Lee Miller
Archives, 1993

But although *Vogue* generally remained aloof from the war, there were a few occasions when this arbiter of feminine taste did confront World War II with a realism that, especially when measured against its usual fare, was sometimes startling. The main instrument for this confrontation was Lee Miller. A member of the magazine's London staff, Miller had once been a much-celebrated fashion model. But under the influence of her onetime lover, the surrealist painter and photographer Man Ray, she had become quite adept with a camera and, in 1940, went to work for *Vogue* as a fashion photographer.

Miller liked fashion photography, had an original flair for it, and had gone to considerable trouble to obtain her position at *Vogue,* including working for the magazine without salary just to prove herself to its editors. Working, however, against the backdrop of wartime London, Miller soon became restive with her assignments. With the evidence of war—from the massive damages wrought on London by German air attacks to the severe shortages in consumer goods—all around her, the thought of spending the war supplying *Vogue* with pictures of expensively clothed models and spreads on the latest in handbags began to seem more trivial than she could bear. Initially Miller found the remedy for her professional malaise in an extracurricular photographic enterprise. The result was a volume entitled *Grim Glory,* the main feature of which was her pictures of bomb-ravaged London.

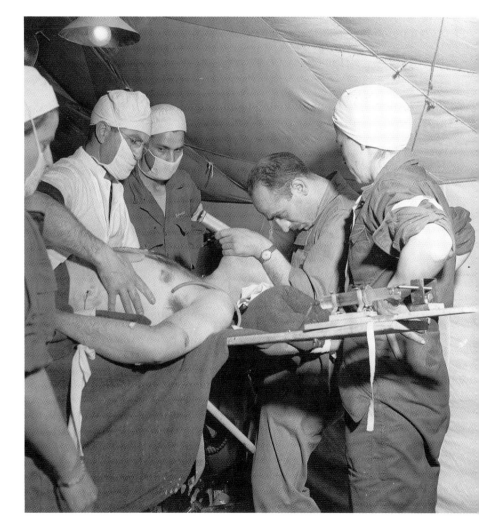

Lee Miller's picture of a pile of dead inmates found at Germany's Dachau concentration camp. Lee Miller, 1945. © Lee Miller Archives, 1993

That piece of work, in turn, whetted Miller's appetite for yet more war-related photography. Before long, she was pressing *Vogue* to admit pictures of World War II into its glossy pages with the understanding, of course, that she would be the one to make them. Ultimately the magazine agreed, but it kept her on a short leash, confining her to war subjects that were thought to be of special interest to its readers, such as American army nurses in Great Britain. The leash, however, gradually lengthened. Shortly after the Allied invasion of Normandy in June 1944, Miller—sporting an army helmet with a raisable front panel of her own devising to facilitate taking pictures—was in France serving as a full-fledged battle correspondent. After producing a remarkably good picture story on the workings of field hospitals, she was on to chronicling the Allied capture, against heavy German resistance, of St. Malo in August.

By then, *Vogue*'s editors had become considerably more amenable to the idea of featuring Miller's war spreads. But they were not prepared for the story that she presented them with in the spring of 1945. Having accompanied American invasion forces into Germany and photographed the historic linkup at the Elbe River between Soviet and American soldiers, she was by late April focusing her camera on the Nazi concentration camps at Dachau and Buchenwald. In submitting her photographs, Miller sensed that *Vogue* would be reluctant to publish her pictorial record of the evidence of human suffering and mass

murder that had taken place in these two camps in the name of Aryan supremacy. She therefore cabled the magazine, imploring it to "believe this is true" and adding that she hoped that it could see its way clear to printing some of them.[15] True or not, *Vogue* did indeed have qualms about carrying the Dachau and Buchenwald pictures, and only after much deliberation and debate did its editors finally go ahead with publishing some of them under the headline "*'BELIEVE IT.'*"[16]

As that emphatically imperative paraphrase of her own cable indicates, Miller felt an acute responsibility to record the massive atrocities of the concentration camps with an unflinching frankness that would leave no question that, incredible as it may seem, they had in fact taken place. As a result, a good many of her pictures were invested with a raw explicitness that made them some of the most effective moral statements on the most heinous chapter in the story of Germany's Third Reich.

# W. EUGENE SMITH

1918–1978

Practically from the moment he first held a camera at age eleven and experienced the click of its shutter, W. Eugene Smith had wanted to be a news photographer. By his early teens, he seldom left his house in Wichita without a camera in hand, and by his senior year of high school, he was regularly supplying Wichita's local newspapers with pictures of community happenings. Within another year, finding that college studies interfered too much with his picture-taking preoccupation, he had dropped out of Notre Dame and launched his career as a full-time photographer in New York City.

Smith, however, did not aspire to practicing just any garden-variety brand of photojournalism. A driven perfectionist whose pursuit of the ideal in his profession would ultimately take on a maniacal quality, Smith early came to believe that it was not sufficient for a news photograph to merely record events. If a picture was to be worthwhile, it must also be a distillation of the meanings and emotions that underlay those events and of its creator's unique perspective on them.

This was a tall order that Smith set for himself, and as a combat photographer in the Pacific during World War II, first for *Flying* magazine and later for *Life,* he was continually bedeviled by thoughts that he was falling short of his goals. Talking in almost mystical terms about his recent photographs of fighting on Saipan in mid-1944, he observed in a letter home: "I am pushing against the wall which is fog and therefore gives and swallows and cannot be pushed. For I am trapped with the puzzle of overcoming war. Dimly, I see my direction, but cannot see the footing, and so far am faltering, and marking time, and bluffing—and failing."[17]

Looking at samplings of Smith's pictures from the Pacific some fifty years later, it is hard to understand this self-flagellation that the photographer regularly inflicted on himself throughout his war correspondent's career. To be sure, not all of his photographs of the American air war and island fighting were great, and it may be that some of them belonged in the category of mere "record" reporting that Smith so wanted to avoid. It may also be that even at their best, his photographs did not meet his idealistic notion of what constituted a good news picture.

That said, Smith did in fact produce some of the most stirring combat photographs of the war, and within his body of work for *Flying* and *Life* were a number of images that have long since become classic embodiments of the texture and sufferings of the war in the Pacific. There is, for example, his brilliantly framed shot of a female Japanese civilian fearfully emerging through smoke with her child from her hiding place on Saipan to confront the island's American conquerors. Then there was his picture of a G.I. gently cradling in his grimy hands a barely breathing Japanese baby that had just been pulled from a

This photograph of Gene Smith most likely dates from his stint on the Pacific aircraft carrier USS *Bunker Hill* in late 1943 and early 1944. Unidentified photographer. Center for Creative Photography, the University of Arizona, Tucson

When writing to his family about this photograph of a wounded soldier on Okinawa, perfectionist Smith rebuked himself at length for not going the extra distance to make it a better picture. To obtain the effect he wanted, he explained, he would have "had to step into the line of fire" that had just felled his subject, and now he was kicking himself for not having done so. W. Eugene Smith for *Life* magazine, 1945. Center for Creative Photography, the University of Arizona, Tucson. © The heirs of W. Eugene Smith

mass of rubble. Remarking on this searing image of one of the most painful realities of war, Smith later wrote: "[The infant's] head was lopsided and its eyes were masses of pus. Unfortunately it was alive. We hoped that it would die."[18] But perhaps the best known of Smith's Pacific photographs was his closely cropped portrayal of a sweat-stained, unshaven, and obviously battle-hardened marine looking warily over his shoulder at the sound of enemy fire. If ever there was a visual distillation of the discomforts and perils of

Pacific island fighting, this is it. Although the rawness of that image prompted censors to forbid its wartime publication, it has since become a classic in American news photography.

In his grail-like quest for perfection in his war pictures, Smith was often indifferent to his own physical safety, and on one occasion he chided himself for letting something as minor as enemy gunfire intimidate him into photographing a wounded soldier from what he later judged to be a less-than-ideal angle. De-

Smith called this picture of a marine on Saipan "one of the best I have made of this war," and he was heartily disgusted when military censors prevented its wartime publication in *Life* because the subject looked too grimy. The image, however, has since come to be regarded as one of the classic photographs of World War II. W. Eugene Smith for *Life* magazine, 1944. Center for Creative Photography, the University of Arizona, Tucson. © The heirs of W. Eugene Smith

scribing Smith's frontline modus operandi, an army public-relations officer who knew him in the Philippines observed: "Gene went beyond dedication. . . . He would take any risk. . . . I followed him around sometimes, and he scared the hell out of me. . . . None of the other photographers had [his] single-mindedness."[19]

In the end that single-mindedness brought a close to Smith's wartime career. Assigned by *Life* in the spring of 1945 to chronicle a day in the life of an average infantryman involved in the taking of Okinawa, Smith pursued his subject—one Terry Moore—with his customary relentlessness. Among the scenes Smith knew he wanted to record was one where Moore came under heavy mortar fire. But "the trouble" with that, Smith later admitted, was "that you have to stand up when anyone with any sense is lying down." And when Moore and the rest of his party did indeed encounter Japanese mortars and Smith rose to record the scene, the inevitable happened: Suddenly Smith, his cam-

This is the picture that Smith was taking when he was hit by enemy fire on Okinawa in the spring of 1945. The wounds to his left hand and mouth were severe, and it was more than a year before Smith used a camera again. W. Eugene Smith for *Life* magazine, 1945. Center for Creative Photography, the University of Arizona, Tucson. © The heirs of W. Eugene Smith

eras smashed, was lying on the ground unconscious, and the first words he heard on coming to were, "Medic, medic, over here, the photographer."[20] Shortly thereafter, he was lying in an army hospital on Guam, the victim of multiple wounds that would require many operations to rectify and that would leave him unable to operate a camera for more than a year.

The cameras Smith had used in this last assignment may have been ruined, but much of his exposed film had survived. In its issue of June 18, 1945, *Life* carried his picture story, "24 Hours with Infantryman Terry Moore," with the text, written in a hospital bed, by Smith himself. Omitted from the spread, however, was a heavily blurred picture of an explosion, which Smith apparently was taking just as he was struck. Doubtless leaving it out met with Smith's approval. After all, important as it might be as a memento of his own life, it was hardly the sort of war photograph that he wanted to be remembered for.

*Opposite page:*
Smith's photograph of a Japanese woman and her child emerging from hiding on Saipan to face the much-feared American soldiers. W. Eugene Smith for *Life* magazine, 1944. Center for Creative Photography, the University of Arizona, Tucson. © The heirs of W. Eugene Smith

## JOE ROSENTHAL
### BORN 1911

In a 1955 article for *Collier's,* chronicling his experiences as an Associated Press photographer covering the marine invasion of Iwo Jima during World War II, Joe Rosenthal introduced himself to his readers as "really just another news photographer."[21] In some respects, that rank-and-file self-characterization was accurate enough. Having begun his photojournalist's career in his late teens, he was currently working for the *San Francisco Examiner,* where he was contentedly employed photographing the Bay Area's local news events. But although Rosenthal's present situation seemed to justify the modest appraisal of himself, even he would have to admit that he was "just another news photographer" with a difference. Of all the thousands of news pictures published in the American press during World War II, none was better known, more celebrated, and more frequently reproduced than his Pulitzer Prize–winning shot of six battle-weary soldiers straining to raise the American flag on Iwo Jima's Mount Suribachi on February 23, 1945. Brilliantly composed, this image possessed every element that a war photograph could want—a dramatic sense of action, sculptural clarity, and heroic patriotism. When the photograph arrived in the United States, it required but one glance on the part of editors to tell them that here was a picture worth featuring prominently.

Joe Rosenthal (*left*) sits with Marine Corps photographer Bob Campbell at the base of Mount Suribachi on Iwo Jima. Behind them is a defunct Japanese gun. Unidentified photographer, 1945. AP/ Wide World Photos

Rosenthal's Pulitzer Prize–
winning photograph of the
flag-raising on Iwo Jima. Joe
Rosenthal, 1945. AP/Wide
World Photos

But the first widespread publication of Rosenthal's flag-raising picture in late February 1945 was almost the least noteworthy manifestation of the admiration it engendered. Returning to the United States shortly thereafter, Rosenthal found that both he and the soldiers involved had become much-honored heroes and were now in great demand for public appearances. More significant, the picture quickly took on a charisma that eventually made it the inspiration for a movie and led to its replication in a multitude of media. Likened by one art critic to Leonardo da Vinci's *Last Supper,* it became the basis for, among other things, war-loan posters, a three-cent stamp, a Rose Bowl float, and sculptor Felix de Weldon's Marine Memorial statue that was unveiled in Arlington, Virginia, in 1954.

Behind Rosenthal's picture is a story fraught with a number of ironies. To begin with, when Rosenthal looked back on his eleven days of recording the battle for Iwo Jima, it was not that image for which he had the greatest professional fondness. Rather it was one taken in the first hours of the invasion. Landing on the island's beaches hard on the heels of the first wave of marines, Rosenthal had found himself, like the armed men around him, dodging a stiff barrage of enemy fire. Seeking picture opportunities while remaining mindful of the need to find cover, he was darting from shell crater to shell crater when he spotted the bodies of two dead marines. In that moment, he conceived the idea for a photograph intended to evoke the essence of what he was witnessing. Thus, bringing the bodies of the two fallen men into his camera's focus, he waited for an advancing marine to come within view, and when one did, he took a picture that, in his estimation at least, embodied the "honest ingredients" of what the Iwo Jima story in its early phases was all about— the dead paving the way so that the living might follow.[22]

Despite the forethought that went into that beach picture, the resulting image did not seemed contrived, which is probably one of the chief reasons why Rosenthal took special pride in it. On the other hand, his picture of the flag-raising on Mount Suribachi four days later—which, in its compositional perfection, did seem contrived and led to conjectures by some that it had to have been carefully posed—was in fact largely a matter of several strokes of extraordinary luck.

Camera used by Rosenthal to take the flag-raising picture on Iwo Jima. George Eastman House, Rochester, New York

This picture of a marine (*far right*) advancing toward the corpses of two fellow soldiers during the early stages of the beach landing on Iwo Jima was a photograph in which Rosenthal took special professional pride. Joe Rosenthal, 1945. AP/Wide World Photos

When everyone started congratulating him on his wonderful flag-raising photograph, Rosenthal at first thought that they must be talking about this post–flag-raising celebration picture. Joe Rosenthal, 1945. AP/Wide World Photos

PUTTING THE WAR IN FOCUS    79

The first bit of good fortune was Rosenthal's decision on February 23 to pursue an unpromising picture opportunity. The battle for Iwo Jima was far from over. By then, however, a successful outcome was assured, and a group of soldiers had been sent that morning to the top of Mount Suribachi to hoist an American flag that would serve as a morale-boosting symbol of certain victory to the soldiers below. But the flag had proven too small for the purpose, and to correct the situation another flag-raising party was organized. Rosenthal had missed the first raising, and when he heard that a second was in the offing, he thought that he would be too late to catch it but that he might as well try to get a few post-raising shots. As it happened, however, he was not too late, and at about noon, he arrived atop Mount Suribachi as soldiers were attaching a considerably larger Stars and Stripes to a heavy iron pole.

Once he was there, Rosenthal's luck continued unabated. As soldiers dug the flag-bearing pole into the ground and pushed the pole upward to a ninety-degree angle, he later recalled, he had unknowingly taken up the perfect position to focus on the scene. And that, combined with the facts that the natural light happened to be neither too weak nor too strong and that a gentle wind happened to be blowing the flag in a compositionally fortunate direction, is what made for the success of his flag-raising picture. Had one of these three factors—wind, positioning, or sunlight—been measurably less favorable, World

War II's most celebrated click of a camera shutter might well have yielded a substantially less satisfactory photograph.

Rosenthal's good fortune on Mount Suribachi is only the most famed example of the chance occurrences that all photographers experienced during World War II and that sometimes led to extraordinarily memorable pictures. Doubtless, all of the photographers who covered that conflict came away from it with stories about how the unpredictable elements of war—from weather to surprise attacks to having one's lens focused in the right direction at the right time—affected the quality of their work. In short, despite a sophistication in camera technology far greater than in any previous war, the photojournalism of World War II was still an inexact science at best. That made for frustration on occasion, but it was also what made photographing the war such an engaging enterprise.

# 4

## NO JOB FOR A WOMAN

By the eve of World War II, the walls of bias that had for centuries blocked women from pursuing professional careers had eroded appreciably. Although the barriers of sexist prejudice still remained largely in place, it was at least no longer entirely unrealistic for a woman to think that she could make her way in such traditionally male-dominated callings as medicine or law or engineering. This went for the field of journalism as well. The day had long since passed when a female reporter was regarded as a contradiction in terms or, for that matter, even as a rare and exotic newsroom aberration who owed her job to some eccentrically open-minded managing editor. Admittedly, news reporting was still mostly a man's world, and it would be many years before women would achieve anywhere near an equal footing with men in that field. Still, the fact remained that by 1940 or so, if a woman was so inclined, it was possible for her to make a go of a journalistic career. What was more, if she was good at her work, it was conceivable that, like investigative reporter Ida Tarbell or widely quoted political columnist Dorothy Thompson, she could win considerable fame as well.

Despite a fair measure of tolerance in journalism, though, there was still one branch of the trade that was deemed ill-suited for a woman: reporting the military operations of World War II. Arguments in defense of that conviction varied according to who was offering them. There were those, for example, who believed that a woman reporter's mind was somehow less capable of understanding war, which, after all, had been defined as strictly a male business since time immemorial. Then there was the chivalric school of thought, which claimed that war presented too many hardships and perils that a woman reporter would not be physically able to endure. Others of a more practical turn of mind argued that providing such amenities as separate field latrines for women combat reporters imposed a

81

*Previous page:*
A group of female correspondents in northern France in the summer of 1944: (*left to right*) Ruth Cowan, Associated Press; Sonia Tomara, *New York Herald Tribune;* Rosette Hargrove, Newspaper Enterprise Association; Betty Knox, Great Britain's *Evening Standard;* Iris Carpenter, *Boston Globe;* Erica Mann, *Liberty Magazine.* United States Army Signal Corps photographer. Still Picture Branch, National Archives, Washington, D.C.

burden on the military that it should not have to bear in the midst of its struggle to subdue the enemy. But whatever the line of reasoning, the outcome was the same. Although it was perfectly acceptable for women reporters to cover war-related news on the home front, there was initially strong reluctance, among editors and military officials alike, to permit female correspondents to venture into actual war zones.

Pitted against the litany of antifeminist arguments, however, were other factors that ultimately led to the emergence of women during World War II as full-fledged war correspondents. For starters, there were a good many women journalists who, regardless of the dangers, were anxious to cover the war's military operations and who, moreover, felt capable of performing that task every bit as intelligently and resourcefully as their fellow male professionals. In short, when United Press war correspondent Ann Stringer later bragged that she "could write the pants off" of any of her male peers, she was expressing a confidence shared by many of her fellow women reporters.[1] But, of course, eagerness on the part of women journalists to engage in war reportage was not in itself enough to break down the prejudices against sending them to theaters of combat. The women also needed a sympathetic boost from various masculine quarters. That came in the form of a growing recognition among both newsroom managers and some military officials that perhaps the so-called woman's angle might be a useful ingredient in the coverage of such phases of World War II as field hospitals and the endeavors of the army and navy's newly established female service branches.

So it was that the hard line against the involvement of women in war reporting began to break down. By 1943 female journalists, though not always without struggle and protracted delays, were gaining accreditation as war correspondents generally with the understanding that their news gathering would be confined mainly to stories found in the rear lines of Allied military operations. But with the door now slightly ajar, the temptation was strong among women reporters to push it wide open, and they quickly began finding opportunities to go beyond the limitations defined in most of their credentials. As a result, by war's end, a good many female journalists had seen and reported on enough frontline combat to qualify themselves as veteran war correspondents in every sense of the word. Furthermore, like all seasoned war reporters, they had in the process accrued their fair share of memorable tales, ranging everywhere from the serendipitous capture of six German soldiers in France by Lee Carson of International News Service to *Collier's* correspondent Martha Gellhorn's hair-raising flight over Germany through a barrage of enemy fire.

The advent of women as frontline correspondents was owing, in large degree, to the initiative of the women themselves, who in their pursuit of a good story were frequently willing to risk disaccreditation by breaking the ground rules that would otherwise have confined them to the safer rear lines. But it was also due to the quality of their performance, which engendered considerable respect among many of the military officers who regulated their comings and goings. Ultimately, that respect led to a more liberal outlook when it came to deciding where female correspondents could or could not go in a given theater of war.

A case in point was *New York Herald Tribune* reporter Sonia Tomara. While stationed in the China-Burma-India theater, Tomara wanted to go on a combat flying mission but had been denied permission to do so by the commanding general, Joseph Stilwell. After obtaining the blessing of Stilwell's subordinate, General Claire Chennault, however, she went anyway, and shortly after her return, she heard that a press officer had cited her for insubordination in a memo to Stilwell. Now fearing that disaccreditation was a distinct possibility, she wrote Stilwell a letter apologizing profusely for going on the flight. As it turned out, however, that was unnecessary. Stilwell thought too well of Tomara to consider banishing her from his jurisdiction. "We like you," he responded, "and it's all right."[2]

Associated Press correspondent Ruth Cowan conducting an interview. Unidentified photographer, 1943. Washington Press Club Archive, National Press Club, Washington, D.C.

## PEGGY HULL DEUELL

1889–1967

Of the many news stories filed by female journalists during World War II, the columns and features produced by Pacific correspondent Peggy Hull Deuell for the

*Cleveland Plain Dealer* and the North American Newspaper Alliance number among the more ephemeral. Indeed, when read today, a good many of her chatty commentaries on encounters with soldiers and the rigors of military life seem trivial and largely forgettable. There was, however, one thing about Deuell that invested her with a special cachet: Unlike most other female reporters of World War II, she was no neophyte when it came to chronicling war. In fact, in demonstrating women's capacity for war reporting, Peggy Hull Deuell was something of a pioneer.

Having begun her journalistic career at age sixteen as a typesetter for a small-town newspaper in her native Kansas, Deuell had experienced her first taste of military action in 1916, when she went to the Texas-Mexico border to cover the American army's attempt to end the cross-border raids of the anti-American Mexican revolutionary Pancho Villa for the *Cleveland Plain Dealer*. She did not see any actual fighting on that occasion, but this glimpse into military life obviously struck a responsive chord in her restless nature. Shortly after the United States became an active participant in World War I in the spring of 1917, Deuell began badgering her then-employer, the *El Paso Morning Times,* to send her to France to report on the American army's role in subduing Germany. Initially, the *Morning Times'* managing editor scornfully dismissed this proposal as "perfectly ridiculous!"—in part because the paper could not afford to send her and in part because she was a woman.[3] Deuell, however, would not take no for an answer. By that summer, she was in Paris preparing to take up her tasks as a roving reporter charged with supplying the *Morning Times* with human-interest stories on the American doughboy in Europe.

Deuell's journalistic endeavors never took her to the front lines of World War I, but her lively accounts of American training camps in France proved something of a sensation. Before long her stories were being picked up by the *Chicago Tribune*'s army European edition, which introduced her to its soldier readership as a "typical young American woman" with "grit and energy."[4]

But Deuell's success as a war correspondent turned out to have its downside when a number of other American papers began carrying her human-interest stories. Heartily irritated by communications from their stateside editors complaining that Deuell was producing more interesting copy on the war than they, some male war correspondents took it on themselves to point out to the army that their female rival from El Paso had never been properly accredited as a war correspondent. Unfortunately for Deuell, the charge was true. By late 1917, unable to win accreditation, she was on her way back to Texas.

Deuell, however, had enjoyed her stay among American troops in France too much to let her career as a war correspondent die. By mid-1918, this time under the auspices of a national news syndicate, she was in Washington lobbying the War De-

partment for permission to cover the American military expedition that had gone to Siberia to protect Czech troops stranded there in the chaotic and still-perilous wake of the Russian Revolution and to facilitate their reunion with other Allied forces on the western front. Despite the War Department's strong reluctance to let a woman venture into this situation, Deuell persisted until permission was finally granted. Although her subsequent trek to Siberia's icy clime in the fall of 1918 produced stories on a sidelight of World War I that had only minimal interest for American newspaper readers, it nevertheless represented a significant

*Opposite:*
Peggy Hull Deuell in the Pacific. United States Army Signal Corps photographer. Kansas Collection, University of Kansas Libraries, Lawrence

This photograph of Peggy Deuell dates from her first experience in covering a military operation, which occurred in 1916 when she traveled to the Texas-Mexico border to cover the United States Army's attempt to put a stop to Pancho Villa's raids on American soil. While there, she went on a fifteen-mile hike with an infantry company and came through it, to use her own proud words, a "hardened veteran." The uniform Deuell wears in the picture was borrowed from the Ohio National Guard. Kehres (lifedates unknown), 1916. Kansas Collection, University of Kansas Libraries, Lawrence

The first press credential ever issued to a woman by the American military—Peggy Hull Deuell's pass allowing her to cover United States operations in Siberia at the end of World War I. Kansas Collection, University of Kansas Libraries, Lawrence

landmark: For the first time in the annals of American journalism, a woman had been officially accredited as a war correspondent.

Unfortunately, being the primary instrument and beneficiary of this feminist breakthrough did not help Deuell a whit when it came to procuring her war correspondent's accreditation for World War II. Instead, when she went to Washington in

the summer of 1943 to pick up her press credentials, it quickly became apparent that she had two strikes against her that, in the War Department's view at least, far outweighed her singular distinction of more than twenty years ago. One, Deuell was now well into her fifties, and as she began making the rounds of War Department offices, she encountered a young officer who told her in effect that she should content herself with observing the current war from a "rocking chair" on "the old front porch."[5] Then there was the fact that Deuell did not want press credentials for just any front. Rather, she was determined to cover the war in the Pacific, whose combat theaters, many military officials thought, did not lend themselves as easily as Europe's to the accommodation of female journalists. Still, Deuell persevered. By late 1943, after a wait of some five months, her papers were finally in order, and she was bound for the Pacific.

Deuell's accreditation, however, did not mean that she was to be permitted to see the war close up. Because of her age and sex, her reporting activities were confined to military bases and hospitals in Hawaii for more than two-thirds of her year-and-a-half stay in the Pacific. Not until January 1945 was she finally allowed to visit some of the islands that had recently been wrested from Japanese control.

Deuell sometimes bridled under the constraints imposed on her, and she was not above airing her dissatisfaction to her readers at home. For her, she wrote in a column of August 1944, there would be "no memories of desperate hours well shared with brave Americans. I am a woman and as a woman am not permitted to experience the hazards of real war reporting."[6] By and large, however, she made the best of her situation, concentrating on small human-interest stories about the soldiers she met and the military installations she saw. Such pieces, she readily acknowledged, would win her "no prize awards," and most would be forgotten soon after they were read. But Deuell's limited brand of war reportage was not quite as negligible as she thought. For, in focusing on the war's daily human texture, she offered a glimpse into this global conflict that often made its meanings a bit more concrete and comprehensible.

## HELEN KIRKPATRICK
### BORN 1909

Following her graduation from Smith College in 1931 and a period of postgraduate study at Switzerland's University of Geneva, Helen Kirkpatrick faced the decision that every young adult must ultimately face—what to do with the rest of her life. In contemplating her choices, a fascination with contemporary history and an interest in writing about it initially led her to journalism and a job interview at the *New York Herald Tribune.* Her encounter with an editor there, however, was at best a qualified success. Although the editor thought well enough of Kirkpatrick to offer her a fourteen-dollar-a-week job, he felt obliged to warn her that a woman's prospects for advancement in journalism were extremely thin. So, weighing the pros and cons of that positive message with its discouraging caveat, Kirkpatrick decided to pass up the opportunity to work for one of New York City's leading dailies. Instead, she turned to a corner of the working world where women seemed to have a better chance for advancement, and she was soon part of a training program at Macy's department store with an eye to making her way in merchandising.

Kirkpatrick did well in the training program and was highly thought of by her supervisor, but there was one significant hitch. Despite a good performance strongly suggesting that she would eventually do well as a Macy's department head

or buyer, her heart was not in it. What was more, it showed. So much so, that a British psychiatrist, who was conducting a behavioral study at the department store, took her aside one day and told her, "You know, this isn't your line."[7]

Ultimately Kirkpatrick had to concede the shrewdness of that judgment, and in 1935 she returned to Geneva, where she found a job as a writer-editor for *Research Bulletin,* a publication put out by the Foreign Policy Association, which was based there. As headquarters for the League of Nations, Geneva was a center for international news of some import, and through her connections with correspondents there, she soon found opportunities to expand her journalistic endeavors. While working for the *Bulletin,* she periodically supplied articles on various international developments to a number of British newspapers, and before long, the fine quality of her reportage gave rise to a brisk demand for her services. Within a year or so of her coming to Geneva, she had quit the *Bulletin* to devote all her time to working as a stringer for an array of papers that included the *Manchester Guardian,* the *London Daily Telegraph,* and the *New York Herald Tribune.*

Kirkpatrick in later years described herself in this early stage of her career as a shy and rather reticent person who often hesitated to draw on a possibly valuable news source for fear of imposing. But apparently that did not prevent her from developing a network of good inside contacts within Geneva's international

Helen Kirkpatrick with Allied forces in Europe. Unidentified photographer for the *Chicago Daily News,* 1944. Reprinted with the permission of the Washington Press Club and Helen Kirkpatrick Milbank. Washington Press Club Foundation, Washington, D.C.

The *Chicago Daily News* early recognized that Helen Kirkpatrick was one of its greatest assets during the war. Thus, in promoting its news service and the daily circulation of the *Daily News,* the paper often made Kirkpatrick the focal point of its advertising. The poster here began appearing at Chicago newsstands shortly after the invasion of Normandy. Sophia Smith Collection, Smith College, Northampton, Massachusetts

Read HELEN KIRKPATRICK'S Reports on the INVASION
THE DAILY NEWS

**HELEN KIRKPATRICK REPORTS SNIPER ATTACK ON FRENCH LEADERS AT NOTRE DAME CATHEDRAL**

PARIS, AUGUST 26, 1944

The Allies had just liberated Paris, and Helen Kirkpatrick was lunching at the city's Ritz Hotel with Ernest Hemingway when she announced that she had to leave to cover the victory parade through Paris. Hemingway told her that their repast at the fabled Ritz was far more historic than the story she intended to cover. Kirkpatrick left anyway. The result was the scoop below.

Paris' celebration of its liberation was very nearly converted into a massacre by the Fascist militia's attempt to eliminate French leaders and to start riots during the afternoon's ceremonies.

All Paris streamed into the center of the town—to the Arc de Triomphe, the Place de la Concorde, along the Champs Elysees, at the Hotel de Ville and to Notre Dame Cathedral.

Gens. De Gaulle, Koenig, Leclerc and Juin led the procession from the Etoile to Notre Dame amid scenes of tremendous enthusiasm.

Lt. John Reinhart, U.S.N., and I could not get near enough to the Arc de Triomphe to see the parade, so we turned back to Notre Dame where a Te Deum service was to be held. . . .

The generals' car arrived on the dot of 4:15. As they stepped from the car, we stood at salute and at that very moment a revolver shot rang out. It seemed to come from behind one of Notre Dame's gargoyles. Within a split second a machine gun opened from a nearby room. . . . It sprayed the pavement at my feet. The generals entered the church with 40-odd people pressing from behind to find shelter.

I found myself inside in the main aisle, a few feet behind the generals. People were cowering behind pillars. Someone tried to pull me down.

The generals marched slowly down the main aisle, their hats in their hands. People in the main body were pressed back near the pillars. . . .

Suddenly an automatic opened up from behind us—it came from behind the pipes of Notre Dame's organ. From the clerestory above other shots rang out and I saw a man ducking be-hind a pillar above. Beside me F.F.I. men and the police were shooting.

For one flashing instant it seemed that a great massacre was bound to take place as the cathedral reverberated with the sound of guns. . . .

It seemed hours but it was only a few minutes, perhaps 10, when the procession came back down the aisle. I think the shooting was still going on but, like those around me, I could only stand amazed at the coolness, imperturbability and apparent unconcern of French generals and civilians alike who walked as though nothing had happened. Gen. Koenig, smiling, leaned across and shook my hand.

I fell in behind them and watched them walk deliberately out and into their cars. A machine gun was still blazing from a nearby roof.

Once outside, one could hear shooting all along the Seine. . . . I learned later that shooting at the Hotel de Ville, the Tuilleries, the Arc de Triomphe and along the Elysees had started at exactly the same moment. . . .

It was a clearly planned attempt probably designed to kill as many of the French authorities as possible, to create panic and to start riots after which probably the mad brains of the militia, instigated by the Germans, hoped to retake Paris.

community and from ferreting out stories. By 1937 her reputation as a capable observer of the comings and goings at the League of Nations had earned her an invitation to come to London to help put out the *Whitehall News,* a weekly newsletter trafficking heavily in the analysis of the current state of European affairs.

In London, Kirkpatrick's star continued to rise as she applied herself to reporting the events of the next two years that would finally plunge Europe into all-out war in September 1939. In interpreting those events—namely Germany's rapid rearmament and unopposed takeovers of Austria and Czechoslovakia—she rankled many within the British establishment with her undisguised disdain for the Anglo-French willingness to accept Hitler's prewar aggressions. As a matter of fact, when Kirkpatrick put her criticism into book form following the Anglo-French acquiescence to Hitler's demands for Czechoslovakia's Sudetenland, Britain's Tory government went so far as to forbid the book's sale in stalls at London's train stations. But British officialdom's distaste for Kirkpatrick's editorial slant did not prevent her from winning plaudits in other quarters. By the time the *Chicago Daily News* took her on as a European correspondent in 1939, she was widely regarded as a remarkably thorough and astute journalist with "the best sources in the business."[8]

When the owner of the *Daily News,* Frank Knox, learned that his London office wanted Kirkpatrick for its staff, he had to overcome a strong aversion to hiring a woman as an overseas reporter before finally giving his blessing to her admission to the paper's payroll. But if Knox continued to harbor fears about Kirkpatrick, they soon evaporated. With the outbreak of war in Europe following Hitler's invasion of Poland, Kirkpatrick soon proved to be worth her weight in gold, and maybe then some. During the nightly German bombings of Great Britain that began the summer of 1940, she rode intrepidly through London's devastated streets in ambulances and fire engines and, from those experiences, produced some of the best coverage in the American press of that phase of World War II.

In the spring of 1940, thanks to her large network of well-placed sources, she also managed to scoop the rest of her profession with her soon-to-be realized prediction that Hitler was poising his armies for an invasion of neutral Belgium. At about the same time, she even scored something of a beat on her boss Frank Knox when, in a front-page column adjacent to one carrying Knox's own emphatic statement to the contrary, the *Daily News* printed Kirkpatrick's prescient hunch that Mussolini would take Italy into the war as Germany's ally by mid-June 1940.

In the war's later stages, Kirkpatrick proved equally adept at covering Allied ground operations as they moved through North Africa, to Italy and France, and finally into Germany. She also won a reputation as a tough, self-sufficient individual who gave lie to the notion that female reporters were too fragile to weather the vicissitudes of frontline reporting without special assistance from the army. When someone at a high-level military staff meeting voiced the opinion that female journalists should be barred from the Normandy invasion because there would be no latrines for them, an admirer of hers offered to bet five British pounds that "Helen Kirkpatrick could dig a latrine faster than anyone in this room."[9] The point was well taken; no one rose to the challenge.

But wide admiration for Kirkpatrick among fellow war correspondents and the military did not guarantee that readers of her dispatches in the *Daily News* always held her in reverence. That was particularly so when her stories began to include her own tactical analysis of battlefront operations. Believing that no feminine mind was capable of making a sound judgment on the Allied military moves, some *Daily News* readers took it on themselves to inform the paper's editors that Kirkpatrick should not be allowed to discuss such an obviously masculine matter. Recalling this campaign to curtail her combat reportage long after the war, Kirkpatrick dismissed the premise for it as "utter nonsense." As for her editors at the *Daily News,* they, too, shared that sentiment. Not only did they refuse to limit the scope of Kirkpatrick's subject matter; they flaunted her reportorial comprehensiveness as a badge of pride. Thus, when Kirkpatrick came to Chicago while on leave from the European front, she found herself accosted by perfect strangers who addressed her by her first name. It was not long before she knew the reason for this amiable familiarity: Her chronicles of the war in Europe had become the centerpiece in the *Daily News*'s circulation promotions, and posters emblazoned with her picture were telling the bus riders of Chicago that the best means for staying informed on the war was to read "Our Helen."[10]

Helen Kirkpatrick's press credential authorizing her to cover the French army's part in the liberation of France. Sophia Smith Collection, Smith College, Northampton, Massachusetts

# 5

# THE WORM'S-EYE VIEW OF THE WAR

## ERNIE PYLE AND BILL MAULDIN

There are many ways to cover a war, and given its magnitude, World War II offered many ways indeed. It was possible, for example, to concentrate on the conflict's politics as the civilian leaders of the warring nations balanced off their particular interests and goals against those of their allies. In following the war's progress on the battlefield, reporters inclined to painting big pictures could write about strategies and tactics and how they were working against the opposition. Meanwhile, their more future-oriented brethren might be concerned primarily, especially as the war entered its final stages, with analyzing the possible postwar implications that a particular military decision was likely to have. Still others might give priority to profiles of generals, admirals, and other high-ranking officers. Finally, another line the reporter could take was to focus on the average combat soldier and what the war was like from his point of view.

Sooner or later, most war correspondents took that last-mentioned tack to one degree or another. But none of them did it more assiduously or to better effect than the syndicated columnist Ernie Pyle and *Stars and Stripes* cartoonist Bill Mauldin. Far more than any others, they were the interpreters of the American enlisted man's experience, and their records of the war—one in words and the other in satiric drawings—were two of the hallmark journalistic achievements of the war.

This photograph of Ernie Pyle (*center*) on Iwo Jima early in 1945 calls to mind a dimension of his *modus operandi* that went a long way in accounting for the freshness of his writing. When he sat down to chat with American GIs, he was disinclined to channel the conversation toward this or that topic. Instead, having no predetermined agenda of his own, he tended to let the inspiration for his pieces more or less bubble up from the free-flowing banter. Sergeant T. D. Barnett, Jr., United States Marine Corps. Still Picture Branch, National Archives, Washington, D.C.

In the summer of 1944, Pyle's phenomenal popularity inspired *Time* to do a cover story on him, and it was for that occasion that artist Boris Chaliapin painted this likeness of him. Pyle was not entirely pleased with the final article. Among its most objectionable aspects was the claim that Pyle's interest in making the average soldier the focus of his columns dated from a moment in North Africa when he sought cover from enemy fire in a foxhole occupied by a dead infantryman. "Nothing remotely resembling that ever happened," Pyle fumed in a letter to his wife. This epiphany-like incident may have been fictional, but it testified to an important truth: Pyle's charisma had made him the stuff of myths. Boris Chaliapin (1904–1979), 1944. Gouache on board, 30.5 x 26.7 cm (12 x 10½ in.). School of Journalism, Indiana University, Bloomington

# ERNIE PYLE
## 1900–1945

Upon spotting him, soldiers were apt, even in combat situations, to set aside the business at hand and crowd around him to ask for his autograph. General Omar Bradley once claimed that whenever he was nearby, his men fought better. His admirers, both in and out of the army, were legion, and fan letters to him sometimes had to be carried in by the wheelbarrow. Congressmen and senators frequently quoted him. In July 1944, he was the subject of a laudatory *Time* cover story, and by 1945 Hollywood had translated his wartime experiences into a movie. When he returned home to the United States for a little respite from war, he was heaped with awards; agents promised him a surefire fortune if he ever decided to go on the lecture circuit; *Life* dispatched one of its top photographers to make a picture of him; and people cruised by his house in Albuquerque, New Mexico, to catch a quick glimpse of him.

No, the object of all this attention and adulation was not some unusually charismatic general. Nor was it some superheroic enlisted man, who in the fashion of Sergeant York had single-handedly subdued a couple of German or Japanese battalions. Rather it was a balding, painfully shy, bantam-weight Hoosier journalist named Ernie Pyle, whose gift for war reportage had earned him a celebrity and universal affection that have never been equaled in the history of American journalism.

But if Pyle's preeminence as a chronicler of World War II seems unassailable in retrospect, no one on the eve of that conflict, least of all the unassuming Pyle himself, would have singled him out as a contender for that distinction. Reared on a farm, Pyle had entered Indiana University in 1919 with no particular vocational ambition. All he knew was that he heartily disliked the rigors of working his family's farm, and that just about anything was better than spending the rest of his life staring "at the south end of a horse going north."[1] Thus, when he enrolled as a freshman in the university's journalism curriculum, he did so not out of any well-defined sense that his proper niche lay somewhere in the Fourth Estate. Rather, he had learned from a friend that journalism courses were a cinch, and they therefore seemed to offer as easy a means as any for escaping the plow. Casual though this initial commitment was, Pyle nevertheless found his classroom exposure to the art of reporting compatible enough. In January 1923, he was leaving the university just a few months short of qualifying for his undergraduate degree to take a reporter's job with a small newspaper in La Porte, Indiana.

Pyle's stay in La Porte was short. Within six months, a connection from his university days helped him to get a job in Washington, D.C., with the *Washington Daily News*. From there he went on to short stints with two newspapers in New York,

and by 1928 he was back at the *Daily News* working as a copy editor. Within another four years, he had become the paper's managing editor. Then, in 1935, Pyle's career took an unexpected turn. To recover his health following a protracted bout of influenza, he took a three-month leave of absence from the *News* to tour the country with his wife. On his return to Washington, he found that the syndicated columnist Heywood Broun was on vacation and that the space normally reserved for Broun's pieces in the *News* was in need of filling. To accomplish that, Pyle composed some columns of his own about his recent travels, and the management of the Scripps-Howard newspaper chain, which owned the *News,* thought well enough of his stopgap effort to ask him to write a travel column for all its papers on a regular basis. Thoroughly enchanted with the prospect of being a roving reporter, Pyle eagerly accepted the offer. The next several years found him crisscrossing the country with his wife—identified in his columns as "that Girl who rides with me"—in search of colorful material.[2]

In taking on this nomadic enterprise, Pyle did not try to cast himself as a cerebral analyst out to enlighten his readers on significant relationships between the life he encountered in his traveling and the larger issues of the day. Given his retiring nature, he also was decidedly uninterested in snagging interviews with the locally prominent. Instead, what he was generally after were glimpses into the everyday life of obscure individuals. The results were breezily chatty vignettes about his encounters with sheepherders and lumberjacks, farmers and hotel bellhops. The modest parameters of Pyle's roving commentaries produced only a modest success. Although subscribers to the Scripps-Howard newspapers found Pyle's writings entertaining enough, attempts to syndicate his column in papers outside of the Scripps chain found no more than a handful of takers.

With the advent of World War II, however, Pyle's no-more-than-middling fortunes began moving upward, first by inches and then by quantum leaps. Initially, he had been too preoccupied with his nomadic pursuits of local color to pay much heed in the late 1930s as Hitler's aggressive grabs for *lebensraum* moved Europe toward a continent-wide conflict. But the German invasion of Poland in September 1939 suddenly changed all that. Shortly after Great Britain and France responded to that event by declaring war on Germany, Pyle was reporting to a friend that his ambition to become a war correspondent was such that he was "just about to bust." Unfortunately, the realization of this new burning desire was slow in coming, and despite the fact that his travel columns now struck him as "silly" and "dull" in comparison to what he might be doing, he had to keep churning them out for awhile.[3] It was not until late 1940 that he finally arrived in England to begin his career as a wartime columnist.

There Pyle experienced his first significant taste of success with his accounts of the devastating effects that the German air force's unrelenting bombing attacks on Great Britain were having on its citizenry. By the time he returned to the United States several months later, his stories had earned a public compliment from no less a reader than Eleanor Roosevelt, a number of new newspapers had begun subscribing to his column, and the *New York World-Telegram* had taken to running his reports on the air blitz on its front page.

However gratifying all this might have been for Pyle, the most impressive chapter in the story of his rise did not really begin to unfold until he and other members of the wartime press landed with American troops in North Africa in November 1942. But when it did, it was impressive indeed. As his daily columns on Allied operations in Africa started finding their way into print back in the United States, Pyle's reputation soared like a meteor. Almost overnight he became the most talked about, sought after, and revered member of his profession. Veteran *Collier's* reporter Quentin Reynolds called him "unquestionably the greatest correspondent in Africa." An editor for the *Indianapolis Times* declared his column "the hottest feature we've got," and an assistant editor whose paper did not have the good fortune to be carrying his column confessed to Pyle, "I wish to God I had you." Meanwhile, *Time* was hailing him as "America's most widely read war correspondent," and the fan mail pouring in to him was becoming far more than he could handle. But perhaps the most singular manifestation of

Pyle's escalating fame was the ordinary soldier's curiosity about him. By the time the Allied campaign in Africa was drawing to its successful close in 1943, the question most commonly asked by enlisted men at the front, whenever they encountered members of the press, was: "Do you know Ernie Pyle?" Quentin Reynolds, in fact, met with that query so often that he claimed that it would be the title of his next book about the war. Even the reticently unpretentious Pyle himself had to admit that he was considered by many "the No. 1 correspondent of the war."[4]

After Africa, Pyle went on to cover the Allied invasion of Sicily and Italy and in mid-1944 was with American forces as they established a foothold on the beaches of Normandy and moved toward driving the Germans from Paris. With each change of venue, his reputation seemed to wax only more. By early 1945, having won a Pulitzer Prize the previous year, this onetime travel columnist, who had once had trouble interesting newspapers in his work, was being carried in nearly four hundred American dailies and close to three hundred weekly publications as well.

The explanation for Pyle's success as a war correspondent had several elements to it. For starters, he had a low-keyed, self-effacing manner of dealing with people that enabled him to elicit the makings of a story in quarters where a more aggressive approach might have failed. Moreover, his days as the roving chronicler of "Mt. Hood and hop ranches" had brought to perfec-

Pyle posed for this bust by Jo Davidson during a much-needed stateside vacation in the fall of 1944. Pyle was lionized on this visit everywhere he went, including Davidson's studio, where he was besieged by a steady stream of admirers. Recalling his three sessions with the journalist, Davidson noted in his memoir that he had never seen so "much love and affection" for one individual. Jo Davidson (1883–1952), 1944. Bronze, height 44.1 cm (17⅜ in.). National Portrait Gallery, Smithsonian Institution, Washington, D.C.; gift of Dr. Maury Leibovitz

tion his remarkable ability to spot story potential in situations that most journalists would have dismissed as too trivial to deal with.[5]

Also contributing to his popularity was the matter-of-fact and sometimes staccato simplicity of his journalistic style, which invested his words with a remarkably graphic sense of the horrors and wastes of the war without being histrionic or maudlin. That is not to say that his columns did not on occasion draw tears.

Reading what became his most famous wartime piece, for example, where the subject was the death of Captain Henry T. Waskow, doubtless many of Pyle's readers wept as they learned about the reaction among Waskow's men to the loss of their leader. But if they did, it was not because Pyle had sought to manipulate their emotions by interjecting his own eulogistically editorial voice. Rather it was because in this piece Pyle had discreetly stationed himself at the sideline and let Waskow's men stoically express their grief in word and action. In doing so, he created a verbal tableau whose power to move rested on its unadorned objectivity.

An equally important ingredient in the success of Pyle's columns was what he once called their "worm's-eye view of the war."[6] To be sure, Pyle did his share of

Foxhole shovel carried by Pyle at the front. School of Journalism, Indiana University, Bloomington

consorting with commanding generals and other high-ranking officers in the course of the war, and he periodically devoted columns to some of them. But his commentaries mainly focused on the average soldier and what the war was like for him. Commenting on that approach, John Steinbeck observed that World War II was really two wars. "There is," he noted, *the war of maps and logistics, of campaigns, of ballistics, armies, divisions, and regiments. . . . Then there is the war of homesick, weary, funny, violent, common men, who wash their socks in their helmets, complain about food, whistle at Arab girls, or any other girls for that matter, and lug themselves through as dirty a business as the world has ever seen and do it with humanity and dignity and courage — and that is Ernie Pyle's war.*[7]

In part, Pyle concentrated on this dimension of the war because, given his own shy, unpretentious nature, he related more readily to the military's rank and file than he did to its strategy-making brass. Ultimately, however, his attraction to the enlisted soldier also lay in a recognition of the sometimes overlooked fact that it was the homesick corporals and privates huddled in their foxholes upon whom the war's outcome so largely depended. Thus, from early on, he felt a sharp sense of obligation to use his column as a vehicle for making known to the home front the pains and discomforts, the fears and griefs that were their lot.

In adopting this focus, Pyle made it his special mission to know the American

G.I. inside and out. As a result, when his unsentimentalizing sensitivity was brought to bear on that subject, his words had a weighty authenticity that eventually gave him an oracular authority. At the same time, his preoccupation with the enlisted man reduced the war to terms that much of his audience appreciated far more than depersonalized reports on the war's overall progress on this or that front. When letters to Pyle from parents of soldiers repeatedly observed, in effect, that "reading your column is like getting a letter from my beloved son," they were expressing a thought that doubtless was shared by legions of others.[8]

In one of his columns from Italy, Pyle undertook to define what the war meant for the frontline soldiers there after months of rugged fighting. "It's the constant roar of engines," he wrote, *and perpetual moving and the never settling down and go, go, go night and day, and on through the night again. Eventually it all works itself into an emotional tapestry of one dull dead pattern—yesterday is tomorrow and Troina is Randazzo and when will we ever stop and, God, I'm so tired!*[9] By the time Pyle wrote that, he knew well of what he spoke. In the pursuit of material for his column, he had shared the life of these soldiers for long stretches, and though not carrying a gun, he, too, was susceptible to the numbing fatigue that inevitably came with being on the front line.

On more than one occasion, that fatigue coalesced with all the scenes of human suffering that he witnessed to make his war correspondent's job more than Pyle could bear. At the same time, his many experiences under fire gave rise to a gloomy foreboding that at some point his luck would run out, and he ultimately became plagued with doubts that he would make it through the war alive. Interestingly enough, these feelings of dread and exhaustion did not seem to affect the quality of his work, and his column on Captain Waskow dates from a period in late 1943, when Pyle was convinced that he was rapidly reaching the point where he could not write one more word about the war.

Nor did Pyle's personal demoralization ever lead him to toy seriously with the possibility of leaving the war. He had become one of the war's institutions. More important, he came to feel that he had an unspoken obligation to the long-suffering soldiers whom he wrote about, and, like them, he was in the war for the duration. "Of course I am very sick of the war and would like to leave it," he noted in a letter to his wife, "and yet I know I can't. I've been part of the misery and tragedy of it for so long that . . . I feel if I left it, it would be like a soldier deserting."[10]

When Pyle returned to the United States in the late summer of 1944 after witnessing the liberation of Paris, he therefore knew that this much-needed respite from war, however much he wished otherwise, must be only temporary. By early the next year, having succumbed to urging from the navy that he cover its operations in the Pacific, he was in San Francisco making final preparations to

When Pyle finished his column on the death of Captain Waskow, he handed it over to a fellow reporter with the comment, "This stuff stinks. I just can't seem to get going again." In fact, his tribute to Waskow was among the most moving pieces of reportage to come out of the war, and the editors at the *Washington Daily News* thought well enough of it to devote their paper's entire front page of January 10, 1944, to it. Courtesy Scripps Howard Newspapers

## ERNIE PYLE'S COLUMN ON THE DEATH OF CAPTAIN WASKOW

At the front lines in Italy, Jan. 10 (By Wireless)—In this war I have known a lot of officers who were loved and respected by the soldiers under them. But never have I crossed the trail of any man as beloved as Capt. Henry T. Waskow of Belton, Tex.

Capt. Waskow was a company commander in the 36th Division. He had been in this company since long before he left the States. He was very young, only in his middle twenties, but he carried in him a sincerity and gentleness that made people want to be guided by him.

"After my own father, he comes next," a sergeant told me.

"He always looked after us," a soldier said. "He'd go to bat for us every time."

"I've never known him to do anything unkind," another one said.

* * *

I was at the foot of the mule trail the night they brought Capt. Waskow down. The moon was nearly full, and you could see far up the trail, and even part way across the valley. Soldiers made shadows as they walked.

Dead men had been coming down the mountain all evening, lashed onto the backs of mules. They came lying belly down across the wooden packsaddle, their heads hanging down on the left side of the mule, their stiffened legs sticking awkwardly from the other side, bobbing up and down as the mule walked.

The Italian mule skinners were afraid to walk beside dead men, so Americans had to lead the mules down that night. Even the Americans were reluctant to unlash and lift off the bodies, when they got to the bottom, so an officer had to do it himself and ask others to help.

The first one came early in the morning. They slid him down from the mule, and stood him on his feet for a moment. In the half light he might have been merely a sick man standing there leaning on the other. Then they laid him on the ground in the shadow of the stone wall alongside the road.

I don't know who that first one was. You feel small in the presence of dead men, and you don't ask silly questions. . . .

We left him there beside the road, that first one, and we all went back into the cowshed and sat on watercans or lay on the straw, waiting for the next batch of mules.

Somebody said the dead soldier had been dead for four days, and then nobody said anything more about him. We talked for an hour or more; the dead man lay all alone, outside in the shadow of the wall.

*  *  *

Then a soldier came into the cowshed and said there were some more bodies outside. We went out into the road. Four mules stood there in the moonlight, in the road where the trail came down off the mountain. The soliders who led them stood there waiting.

"This one is Capt. Waskow," one of them said quickly.

Two men unlashed his body from the mule and lifted it off and laid it in the shadow beside the stone wall. Other men took the other bodies off. Finally, there were five lying end to end in a long row. You don't cover up dead men in the combat zones. They just lie there in the shadows until somebody else comes after them.

The uncertain mules moved off to their olive groves. The men in the road seemed reluctant to leave. They stood around, and gradually I could sense them moving, one by one, close to Capt. Waskow's body. Not so much to look, I think, as to say something in finality to him and to themselves. I stood close by and I could hear.

One soldier came and looked down, and he said out loud:

"God damn it!"

Another one came, and he said, "God damn it to hell anyway!" He looked down for a few last moments and then turned and left.

Another man came. I think he was an officer. It was hard to tell officers from men in the dim light, for everybody was grimy and dirty. The man looked down into the dead captain's face and then spoke directly to him, as tho he were alive:

"I'm sorry, old man."

Then a soldier came and stood beside the officer and bent over, and he too spoke to his dead captain, not in a whisper but awfully tender, and he said:

"I sure am sorry, sir."

Then the first man squatted down, and he reached down and took the Captain's hand, and he sat there a full five minutes holding the dead hand in his own and looking intently into the dead face. And he never uttered a sound all the time he sat there.

Finally he put the hand down. He reached up and gently straightened the points of the Captain's shirt collar, and then he sort of rearranged the tattered edges of his uniform around the wound, and then he got up and walked away down the road in the moonlight, all alone.

The rest of us went back into the cowshed, leaving the five dead men lying in a line, end to end, in the shadow of the low stone wall. We lay down on the straw in the cowshed, and pretty soon we were all asleep.

This first marker erected at the site of Pyle's death on Ie Shima was replaced in the summer of 1945 with a small stone monument bearing the same inscription. United States Army Signal Corps photographer. Still Picture Branch, National Archives, Washington, D.C.

reassume his role as America's foremost war correspondent. "I'm going simply because there's a war on and I'm part of it," he wrote. "I'm going simply because I've got to, and I hate it."[11]

Gradually, however, Pyle's spirits lifted as he fell to fraternizing with sailors. By the time he accompanied a group of marines on their landing at Okinawa early in April, he was beginning to take a decidedly more optimistic view of his work. Even the premonitions of his own death began to fade, and shortly after his Okinawa sortie, he observed in a letter, "I feel now that at last I have a pretty good chance of coming through the war alive."[12] Then, on April 17, he arrived on the recently occupied island of Ie Shima and the next day set out with some soldiers in a jeep to survey the terrain, which still contained pock-ets of Japanese resistance. Suddenly the party encountered enemy fire, and its members were soon running for cover. A few moments later, Pyle was dead.

The sense of grief spawned by this event is hard to calculate. Suffice it to say that many mourned the loss of Pyle with a depth of feeling that was not much different from that engendered by the death of President Franklin Roosevelt but a few days earlier. Nowhere was his death more lamented than among American soldiers, whose chronicler he had been from Africa to Normandy and finally to Ie Shima. For evidence of that, it is necessary to look no further than the crudely painted marker that soldiers erected where Pyle had fallen. "AT THIS SPOT," it read, "THE 77TH INFANTRY DIVISION / LOST A BUDDY / ERNIE PYLE / 18 APRIL 1945."[13]

# A LITERARY EVENT

## RICHARD TREGASKIS'S *GUADALCANAL DIARY*

When an army plane dropped International News Service correspondent Richard Tre-gaskis (1916–1963) off in Hawaii in the fall of 1942, he was carrying with him the makings of one of the more noteworthy literary events of World War II. Through most of August and September, this six-foot-seven, Harvard-educated journalist had been on Guadalcanal in the Solomon Islands, where he had witnessed the early stages of the first major, and ultimately successful, Allied offensive against an important Japanese Pacific stronghold. Like any reporter charged with covering such an event, Tregaskis had made copious notes of all that he had seen and heard on Guadalcanal, from the first landing of United States Marines on August 7 through the Battle of Bloody Ridge, where Marines repulsed a major Japanese drive to recapture the island's single most important asset, its airfield.

Pages from one of Tregaskis's Guadalcanal notebooks, with quick notations about the first hours of the invasion. Richard Tregaskis Collection, Department of Special Collections, Mugar Memorial Library, Boston University, Massachusetts

When Tregaskis first started keeping these notes, he doubtless regarded them as little more than an aid in composing his daily dispatches. But at some point the idea for a book set in, and by the time he landed in Hawaii, he had already begun shaping his notebook memoranda into *Guadalcanal Diary*, one of the most widely read frontline accounts to come out of the war.

Ultimately the inspiration for a movie of the same name, *Guadalcanal Diary* by no means represented the final word on the battle actions that it chronicled. Thanks largely to a deceptively affable navy censor in Hawaii who, according to Tregaskis years later, "hacked away" at his final manuscript "with pencil and scissors," the book failed to include many significant aspects of the Guadalcanal struggle—among them the navy's deplorable failure to ensure ample supplies to the marines on the island. But what this volume may have lacked in comprehensiveness, it made up for in its vignettes bringing the wartime reader face to face with the tragic grimness of battle.

*Guadalcanal Diary*'s most engaging dimension, however, lay in its glimpses into the manners, mores, and badinage of the ordinary American combat soldier. "This afternoon trucks came to dump a pile of gray canvas sacks at Col. Hunt's CP," Tregaskis noted at one point. *It was mail—the first to reach the troops since we landed on Guadalcanal! Each man seemed as happy as if you had given him a hundred-dollar bill at the mere thought of getting mail. . . . I saw a circle of marines clustered about one of the lads who had a reputation for being a demon with the gals. These, he said, were letters from his Number One girl. "That's the only dame he could never make," said one of his admirers good naturedly. "He wants to marry her."* Doubtless, it was the humanizing quality of passages such as this one that was largely responsible for making Tregaskis's chronicle a best-seller in 1943 and explained as well why, even a quarter of a century later, many of the country's bookstores continued to keep it in stock.

By the summer of 1943, Tregaskis was covering the Allied invasion of Italy where, along with fulfilling his daily reporting responsibilities to INS, he was compiling material for a second published war diary. Ultimately titled *Invasion Diary*, this book ended with an unexpected twist. While Tregaskis was observing some mountain fighting north of Naples in November 1943, a German shell tore a hole in his skull, and the last pages of *Invasion Diary* chronicle its author's memories of that harrowing and nearly fatal experience.

Richard Tregaskis (*left*) with Marine Major General Alexander Vandegrift on Guadalcanal. Unidentified photographer, 1942. UPI/Bettman Archives

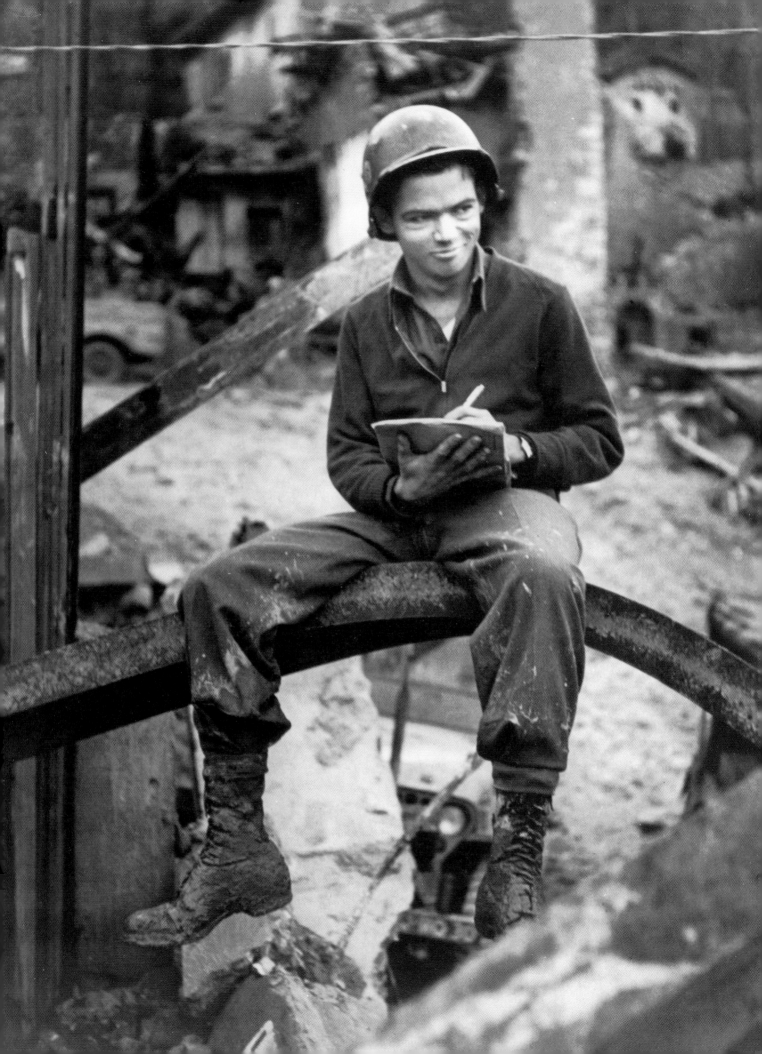

## BILL MAULDIN
### BORN 1921

In early May 1945, the world learned that the annual Pulitzer Prize in editorial cartooning had gone to one Sergeant Bill Mauldin. In traveling down the path to that much-coveted honor, this pucklike twenty-three year old had begun his journey in a rather unorthodox way, to say the least: He had joined the army.

Born in New Mexico, where he had grown up on the edge of poverty, Mauldin had set his sights on the cartooning profession ever since his early teens, and one of his teachers had agreed that his vocational ambitions seemed uniquely well-suited to his rebellious, wisecracking ways. But after leaving high school a quarter-credit short of a diploma, and after a year of training at the Chicago Academy of Fine Art, Mauldin did not fare any too well when he returned to the Southwest to make his way as a pictorial satirist. So, in the fall of 1940, with his prospects in civilian life dim and the possibilities for American involvement in the war in Europe growing ever more certain, he decided to enlist in the army. Soon after, he was serving as a twenty-one-dollar-a-month private in a quartermaster unit of the Forty-fifth Infantry Division.

That did not mean, however, that Mauldin had given up on his original ambitions. To the contrary, in joining the army, he had secretly harbored the hope that somehow he could work an angle that would also permit him to indulge his inclinations for funny drawings. After a few fits and starts, that is exactly what happened. Having advertised his talents for pictorial satire by drawing caricatures of his fellow servicemen at a quarter a throw, he then composed a letter lauding his cartoon talents to an officer who was in the process of setting up a newspaper for the Forty-fifth. Sent off over the signature of one of his buddies, the letter had its desired effect, and he was soon drawing cartoon commentaries on army life for the *45th Division News* on a part-time basis. By the summer of 1943, when he was packed off to the Mediterranean, where the Forty-fifth was slated to participate in the invasions of Sicily and Italy, his cartoon-making responsibilities for the *News* had become a full-time proposition.

In Italy, Mauldin's by-then considerable skills in lampooning military life grew yet more formidable in the midst of combat, and his ability to find humor in the drudgery and hazards of war was soon winning appreciative attention in quarters that went well beyond the soldier readership of the *News.* Before long the European editions of the army's daily, *Stars and Stripes,* were publishing his work, and by early 1944 he had moved from the staff of the *News* to the *Stars and Stripes.* But the enlargement of Mauldin's audience did not end there. Through columnist Ernie Pyle, who had written a flattering column about him, Mauldin had, shortly after his shift to *Stars and Stripes,* been picked up by United Feature Syndicate, and by the sum-

As this photograph of him indicates, Mauldin, unlike his cartoon characters Willie and Joe, was always clean shaven. Taken in Italy, the picture appeared in *Life,* February 5, 1945, in tandem with an article that characterized Mauldin's humor as "both corrosive and compassionate." John Phillips (born 1914) for *Life* magazine. Courtesy John Phillips. © John Phillips

This cartoon, picturing a battle-weary Joe escorting German prisoners to the rear, carried a caption that took the form of a "News Item" and that read: "'Fresh, spirited American troops, flushed with victory, are bringing in thousands of hungry, ragged, battle-weary prisoners.'" The object of the barb was the stateside press, which sometimes sugarcoated the dreary frontline realities of the war with an upbeat rhetoric. This is the cartoon that won Mauldin the Pulitzer Prize. Bill Mauldin, 1944. Pen and ink drawing on paper, 27.3 x 20.3 cm (10¾ x 8 in.). Pulitzer Prize Office, Columbia University, New York City. © 1944 Bill Mauldin. Reprinted with permission

mer of 1944 his work was being carried in scores of newspapers back in the United States.

In large part, Mauldin's phenomenal rise as a cartoon chronicler of the war rested on the stooped shoulders of two un-shaven, hollow-eyed infantrymen, generi-cally known as dogfaces and individually as Willie and Joe. This long-suffering, be-draggled pair were not real people. Rather, they were the two main characters through whom Mauldin spoke in his cartoons; the pug-nosed Joe was more or less the fic-tional alter ego of his creator, and his Roman-nosed friend Willie bore a strong physical resemblance to Mauldin's father. But if Willie and Joe were not made of ac-tual flesh and blood, their often dark-humored running commentary on their soldier's lot, as they intrepidly slogged their blister-footed way through the mud and ruins of war-torn Europe, nevertheless invested them with an endearing and al-most palpable vitality.

And in one sense they were very real in-deed. Through their resigned philosophiz-ing about themselves, their jabs at the privileged existence of officers, their sar-donic reactions to rear-echelon officers and MPs objecting to their unsoldierly posture and dress, and their sometimes na-ively ludicrous efforts to introduce ame-nities to their hard frontline existence, they gave expression to feelings and im-pulses widely shared by enlisted men. But the secret of Willie and Joe's allure was not just the authenticity of their perspec-tive. In serving as a mirror for the discom-

forts, gripes, and perils of the ordinary foot soldier, Mauldin's battle-weary duo had a habit of venting their feelings in a benevolently acerbic way that engendered more laughter than indignation. In so do-ing, they served as a tension-releasing safety valve for their dogface counterparts in real life.

The authenticity of Willie and Joe was no accident. Although his attachment to a newspaper staff formally removed him from any combat roster, Mauldin was smart enough to know that the success of his cartoons hinged on not allowing him-self to become too far removed from the life of the typical combat soldier. Throughout the war, therefore, he regu-larly spent extended periods at the front fraternizing with enlisted men and taking in situations ripe for satirization. When he had soaked up enough background mate-rial to last him for awhile, he would retreat to his drawing board, where he worked up his next batch of cartoons.

In following this procedure, Mauldin inevitably became an active participant in the world he portrayed, and on many occa-sions the source for his work was his own experience. A good case in point was a cartoon captioned "Breakfast in Bed," which featured a prone, bleary-eyed Joe awaking from a night's sleep in an Italian farmer's barn, only to find the udders of a cow staring him in the face. Writing later of the night that inspired this image, Mauldin claimed that it ranked among the finest sleeping experiences he had ever had at the front. Best of all, however, when

This cartoon, *Breakfast in Bed,* was inspired by Mauldin's own experience in Italy of sleeping in a barn and waking up to find a cow hovering over him. Bill Mauldin, not dated. Pen and ink drawing on paper, 26.7 x 20.3 cm (10½ x 8 in.). United States Army Center of Military History, Washington, D.C. © 1944 Bill Mauldin. Reprinted with permission

he awoke to find his improvised bedroom shared by a cow, he lost no time in taking advantage of the situation. Summoning up one of the skills he had acquired back on his family's farm in New Mexico, he was soon milking his intruder and savoring the first fresh milk he had tasted since leaving the United States.

One of the best pieces drawn from Mauldin's experience was a cartoon showing a slumped Willie standing before a first-aid clerk who seeks to present him

with the Purple Heart. Captioned "'Just gimme a coupla aspirin. I already got a Purple Heart,'" the drawing had its origin in Mauldin's visit late in 1943 at a frontline position of a Forty-fifth Division infantry company that had dug itself into some rugged mountainous terrain above an Italian village. While there, he caught the fragment of a German mortar in his right shoulder. The shock of the mortar's explosion left Mauldin thinking for a few seconds that he had been blinded, and the wound itself "burned like fury." But on close examination it proved to be little more than a minor cut. That, however, did not prevent one of the medical assistants who treated it from pressing on him a Purple Heart. Mauldin was taken aback by this attempt to commemorate his scratch and initially rejected the medal, which he thought was reserved for soldiers who had spilled considerably more blood than he had. But the medic was not about to take no for an answer. "The rules say if the enemy draws blood, you get one," he matter-of-factly informed Mauldin. Against that argument, Mauldin's modesty could not prevail.[14] Regulations were regulations, it seemed. Without further protest, he pocketed the medal, mailed it home to his wife, and produced one of his most richly ironic commentaries on the war.

Mauldin has claimed that in drawing his cartoons he was always playing to the frontline enlisted man who followed his work in the *45th Division News* and *Stars and Stripes,* and that his commentaries on the war were meant to boost their morale

Captioned "Just give me th' aspirin. I already got a Purple Heart," this commentary on the ease with which a Purple Heart could be earned was in-spired by the presentation of that medal to Mauldin him-self on the occasion of his slight wounding in Italy. As reproduced in *Bill Mauldin's Army* (New York, 1951). © 1944 Bill Mauldin. Re-printed with permission

by making them laugh at their own condi-tion. If he achieved that end, he did not much care about anything else. But, while the fighting soldier remained his most im-portant audience, there were a great many others who appreciated his work as well. Thus, although his cartoons trafficked heavily at times in insider jokes that only a combat veteran could fully appreciate, they nevertheless won him legions of ci-

In this cartoon the bespecta-
cled soldier remarks to Willie, "This is th' town my
pappy told me about." When
Mauldin made this cartoon,
he had in mind his father's
sometimes racy stories about
serving in France during
World War I. Mauldin later
found out that his father was
not at all gratified to know
that he was the inspiration for
one of his son's jokes, at least
not this one. Bill Mauldin,
not dated. Pen and ink drawing on paper, 28.6 x 22.7 cm
(11¼ x 8¹⁵⁄₁₆ in.). 45th Infantry Division Association,
Oklahoma City. © 1944 Bill
Mauldin. Reprinted with permission

A much favored topic in
Mauldin's pictorial commentaries was aching, poorly
shod, waterlogged feet—a
phenomenon that frontline
soldiers in Europe knew all
too well. His cartoon, "Tell
the ol' man I'm sittin' up wit'
two sick friends," was but
one of several that he did on
the subject. Bill Mauldin, not
dated. Pen and ink drawing
on paper, 28.6 x 22.7 cm
(11¼ x 8¹⁵⁄₁₆ in.). 45th Infantry Division Association,
Oklahoma City. © 1944 Bill
Mauldin. Reprinted with permission

vilian admirers following their syndica-
tion back in the United States. Toward the
war's end, for example, Willie and Joe had
become such a living presence in the life
of one Ohio housewife that with peace
near at hand she was now "dying to see
how" this duo would fare in civilian life.[15]

Mauldin fretted sometimes that because
so many of his barbs were directed
squarely at officers overly preoccupied
with spit, polish, and maintaining their
own rarefied privileges, his cartoons
would not please high-ranking officers.
But despite the anti-authoritarian tinge of
so much of his work, he generally managed to remain in good repute in places
where it counted. Numbered among his
greatest fans, for example, was Italian
front commander General Mark Clark,
who went so far on one occasion as to ask
Mauldin for an original drawing and to
have the cartoonist assigned to his own
jeep—a perquisite hardly ever accorded
to a noncommissioned officer.

Still, Mauldin's periodic worries about
causing displeasure in high places were
not entirely groundless. When, for instance, he produced some cartoons lampooning the sometimes officiously overzealous MPs charged with maintaining
order in occupied rear areas, one general
"hit the gold-leaf ceiling of his baroque
office."[16] In the view of this rules-minded
officer, such satire was totally out of order,
and at a meeting with other high-ranking
officers, he vehemently urged that something be done to curb Mauldin's insolent
wit. Fortunately for Mauldin, most of the

general's audience did not see it that way,
and after letting him sputter on for awhile,
his listeners simply let the matter drop.

Mauldin's most noteworthy scrape with
army brass came early in 1945, when General George Patton wrote a letter to the editors of *Stars and Stripes* threatening to
ban the newspaper from his entire Third
Army if it did not stop carrying Mauldin's
scurrilous attempts to undermine military
discipline. As far as this punctilious, hell-
for-leather, three-star general was concerned, everything about Mauldin's cartoons was objectionable, from the scruffy,
unsoldierly bearing of Willie and Joe to
their less-than-positive attitude toward officers. If no one else saw fit to save the
army from the mutinous sentiments of
Mauldin's cartoons, then Patton would
have to do it himself.

Given Mauldin's enormous popularity
among the rank and file, however, had Patton actually taken steps to curtail the circulation of *Stars and Stripes,* he doubtless
would have done more harm than good
both to himself and to army morale. Patton's superior, Europe's Allied commander
General Dwight Eisenhower, knew that.
Thus, in the interest of saving his favorite
fighting general from making a fool of
himself, Eisenhower had his aide, naval
Captain Harry Butcher, set up an interview between Mauldin and Patton where,
with no references to their respective
ranks, the sergeant and the general could
work out their differences man to man. At
the outset, Mauldin was wary about such
a proposition, but with reassurances from

This cartoon, captioned "My, sir—what an enthusiastic welcome!" was one of the drawings that convinced General Patton that Mauldin was intent on stirring up mutiny in the ranks. Bill Mauldin, not dated. Pen and ink drawing on paper, 28.6 x 22.7 cm (11¼ x 8¹⁵/₁₆ in.). 45th Infantry Division Association, Oklahoma City. © 1944 Bill Mauldin. Reprinted with permission

Butcher that Patton could be a surprisingly open-minded fellow sometimes, he finally consented. In late March 1945, dressed as immaculately as any soldier could be, Mauldin was on his way to meet his most passionate critic at the latter's palace headquarters in Luxembourg.

Captain Butcher's vision of a conciliatory interchange between cartoonist and general did not quite square with the reality. Passing through the imposing double doors of Patton's office and across acres of plush carpeting to the general's desk, Mauldin saluted his host and took a proffered chair, lately vacated by Patton's none-too-friendly bull terrier. With the amenities over, Patton soon launched into a lecture on the history of army discipline and the certain perils of allowing the common soldier too free a rein in speaking his mind. "For a while it was fascinating," Mauldin later recalled. "Patton was a real master on his subject. . . . I felt truly privileged, as if I were hearing Michelangelo on painting. . . . I felt whatever martial spirit was left in me being lifted out and fanned into flame."[17]

Then Patton turned to the subject at hand. Pulling from a drawer some clipped samples of Mauldin's work, he asked their creator to justify their anti-officer tone. In doing so, Mauldin thought he acquitted himself fairly well. By making soldiers laugh at their grievances and letting them know that someone else understood them, he said in effect, he was helping them to let off steam in a relatively harmless way and thereby preventing the mutiny that Patton was so sure he was causing. Patton was clearly unconvinced. "You can't run an army like a mob," he declared when Mauldin was done, and after a handshake and a smart parting salute from Mauldin, the interview was over.[18]

Waiting for Mauldin as he left Patton's office was the *Time* reporter Will Lang who, knowing that this confrontation was taking place, had made it a point to be there when it was over. To Lang's questioning about how the meeting went, Mauldin replied, "I came out with my hide on. We parted friends, but I don't think we changed each other's mind."[19] Mauldin was more or less sanguine about this indecisive outcome. Patton, however, was not. When this general, for whom winning was everything, heard about Mauldin's statement to Lang after it appeared in *Time,* he took it as just one more indication of Mauldin's unpatriotically benighted nature. "If that little s.o.b. ever comes in the Third Army area again," he exploded, "I'll throw him in jail."[20]

History does not record whether Patton was ever aware that about a month later "that little s.o.b." became the recipient of a Pulitzer Prize. But if he was, one can easily imagine his chagrin. Not only did Mauldin have the audacity to disagree with him; one of America's most prestigious professional institutions had now seen fit to honor that waywardness. Had Patton been more sensitive to the egalitarian ethos of the country that he was fighting for, however, he might have realized that his quarrel with Mauldin was one that he could never win. As Mauldin put it years later, when "three stripes go up against three stars" in such matters, "you know three stripes are going to win. [Patton] couldn't win this battle, and he shouldn't have started it."[21]

# 6

# BROADCASTING THE WAR

## EDWARD R. MURROW AND WILLIAM L. SHIRER

Blue Network radio corre-
spondent George Hicks interviewing some sailors shortly
before his historic broadcast
off the French coast on the invasion of Normandy. United
States Navy photographer,
1944. Still Picture Branch,
National Archives, Washington, D.C.

Ask a news editor about his or her idea of a journalistic paradise, and the reply might well be that the best of all possible worlds is one where all the important news of a given day was timed to meet press deadlines. Of course, in the real world things do not work out that way, and all too often the deaths of world leaders and cataclysmic disasters occur without consideration for whether it will be possible to report them fully in the final edition of a given magazine or newspaper.

For many years, American journalism's answer to the unpredictable timing of news events was the hastily printed one- or two-page extra that featured accounts of important late-breaking news and that was rushed to the streets for quick distribution to the public. By the late 1930s, however, a mutation was under way in the country's news-communication industry that was robbing the extra of its purpose and that would eventually relegate it to the same fate as the proverbial dodo bird.

The site of that mutation was network radio. During radio's days of infancy back in the 1920s, those nurturing its growth had tended to regard it as primarily a vehicle for entertainment. As a result, little effort was expended in providing radio audiences with news coverage. By 1930 or so, the regularly scheduled news programming offered by radio's two national networks, NBC and CBS, consisted mainly of one brief evening newscast per network, aired five nights a week. Over the next several years, however, the inclination to give news programming short shrift weakened markedly in the face of indications that listeners liked getting their news over the airwaves and that, as radio expanded its news coverage accordingly, they seemed to like it even more.

So it was that the newspaper extra began to bite the dust. As radio took to exercising with ever greater frequency its superior capacity to air important news practically as soon as it occurred, that journalistic institution found itself shorn of its *raison d'être*.

But when it came to measuring just how far radio newscasting had come by the late 1930s, the decline of the newspaper industry's extra was only the tip of the iceberg. As network radio beefed up its newscast programming and explored its capacities for the live transmission of news from overseas commentators, the news-consuming habits of the American public underwent a change that was both qualitative and quantitative. By 1940, roughly 83 percent of the nearly thirty-five million households in the United States had radios. More to the point, these households, which had once relied exclusively on print journalism for staying abreast of events in the world, were fast becoming accustomed to accomplishing that end aurally. Whereas poll studies of 1938 indicated that a majority of people still regarded their daily newspaper as their main source of news, polls taken three years later showed that radio had emerged as America's news medium of preference.

What was more, radio newscasting seemed to be single-handedly creating a broadly based, well-informed public in corners of the country where none had existed before. During a 1940 tour of the rural West, for example, where poor access to good urban newspapers had until recently tended to keep awareness of happenings in the world at large to a minimum, Bernard De Voto was astonished at the residents' easy conversance with current global events. And what was the source of this unexpected enlightenment? Without a doubt, De Voto claimed, it was radio.

In light of its growing influence as a news medium, it is no surprise that radio came to play an important part in the news coverage of World War II. In fact, in at least one respect, there is some justification for claiming that its role in the journalistic scheme of things was quite possibly pivotal. For, although the exact impact of radio's coverage of World War II, between its outbreak in 1939 and this country's entry into the war two years later, would be difficult to calculate, one thing seems certain: The immediacy of airwave journalism's reportage of the war's early phases bred a sense of personal involvement among Americans. One of the earliest indications of that development came in the wake of Hitler's march into Poland and the outbreak of all-out war in Europe in September 1939. In an article headlined "War in the Living Room," *Newsweek* credited radio's play-by-play coverage of these events with "creating a tension in America undreamed of when the [First] World War broke out in 1914."[1] But what *Newsweek* could not fully appreciate was that this tension marked radio newscasting's arrival as a potent shaper of opinion. Over the next two years, its coverage of the war would be instrumental in promoting a popular climate that was increasingly favorable to active United States involvement in that conflict.

Equally noteworthy was the extent to which radio could sometimes heighten the battlefront realities of World War II for its listeners. In the case of a newspaper account of a given battle—no matter how dramatically and colorfully worded the piece might be—the printed page posed something of a barrier to the reader when it came to comprehending the event's full texture. Radio news reports, on the other hand, often penetrated that barrier, particularly on those occasions when they emanated from an actual battlefront.

Perhaps the single most dramatic example of that occurred the first day of the Normandy invasion, when Blue Network correspondent George Hicks stood on the deck of an American naval ship and, speaking into a portable recorder over the cacophonous din of low-flying enemy planes and antiaircraft guns, offered a running description of the downing of a German plane. *Newsweek* hailed Hicks's performance as the "most realistic report yet to come out of the European war."[2] Some might have thought the compliment a trifle overblown. Still, Hicks's broadcast was the quintessential demonstration of radio's special capacity for making its news-hungry civilian listeners back in the States feel almost as if they were witnessing the war firsthand.

From a rainy beach on the Filipino island of Leyte, General Douglas MacArthur announces via radio the return of American forces to Filipino soil in his famous "I have returned" speech, October 20, 1944. Unidentified photographer, 1944. General Douglas MacArthur Memorial, Norfolk, Virginia

# EDWARD R. MURROW

1908–1965

Like all branches of historical study, there are a variety of ways to approach the story of radio newscasting during World War II, and any two historians writing on that subject are bound to come at their task from quite different angles. But no matter how far apart they might be, on at least one point there is no room for disagreement: Of the many radio newscasters who reported the war, none was more listened to or more celebrated and revered than Edward R. Murrow.

Curiously enough, in 1935 when CBS hired Ed Murrow away from his position as assistant director at the Institute of International Education, the network was not in the least interested in exploring the newscasting capabilities of his authoritative baritone voice. Instead, what had drawn CBS to this darkly handsome and personable young man were his obvious skills as a managerial coordinator. As a result, Murrow spent his first year and a half at CBS as its director of Talks and Special Events. By the spring of 1937, he was on his way to England, charged with the behind-the-scenes orchestration of the network's special broadcasts from Europe, which were to include sports events, concerts, news reports, and talks by noted political and literary figures.

Headquartered in London, Murrow adapted well to this overseas assignment, and as he traveled through Europe devel-

Pictured here with Murrow (*center*) is army air force officer Colonel Joe Kelly (*right*), who piloted ten of the more than twenty combat missions that Murrow flew on during the war. Murrow's superiors at CBS, thinking that it would enhance the authenticity of his reporting, agreed that it would be good for him to go on one or two bombing raids to get a sense of what modern air war was all about. He was, however, too valuable an asset to be risking his neck continually in such adventures, and eventually CBS ordered him to stop going up. To the network's chagrin, he went right on flying anyway. Unidentified photographer, not dated. Murrow Center, Fletcher School of Law and Diplomacy, Tufts University, Medford, Massachusetts

oping useful contacts and lining up programs for CBS, it seemed to all concerned, including Murrow himself, that he had found his proper niche in radio. But on March 11, 1938, events began taking a turn that would suddenly and drastically alter that perception.

On that day, word reached Murrow in Warsaw, where he had gone to arrange for a concert broadcast, that Hitler's strategy of threats and intimidation had made the annexation of Austria to Germany a *fait accompli.* Needless to say, the concert broadcast quickly lost its significance. Murrow's top priority now was to facilitate, as quickly as possible, a European newscast on Hitler's bloodless Austrian conquest, which, among the more prescient, was already regarded as a disturbing harbinger of more German territorial aggressions to come. The most desirable place for this broadcast was Vienna. Unfortunately, Hitler's minions in the Austrian capital would not permit that, so Murrow settled for the next-best thing: Talking the problem through by phone with William L. Shirer, CBS's Vienna-based second-in-command for European programming, it was decided that Shirer should fly to London, where he was to broadcast to America his firsthand account of Hitler's Austrian *Anschluss.* Meanwhile, Murrow would go to Vienna to see what he could do about arranging for a later newscast from there, if the German authorities would allow it.

At CBS headquarters in New York, however, a far grander scheme for cov-ering the *Anschluss* was percolating. In the late afternoon of March 13, Shirer, now in London, and Murrow, in Vienna, learned that their New York bosses wanted them to orchestrate a half-hour "news roundup," consisting of live reports from London, Vienna, Berlin, Paris, and Rome on the reaction in those European capitals to the *Anschluss.* Moreover, New York wanted the program to be ready for airing that very day at 8:00 P.M., American East Coast time. Given time differences between Europe and the United States, that gave Murrow and Shirer some eight hours to deliver the goods.

At first blush, the task seemed altogether impossible. Although roundups had been done before, they had never been organized on such short notice. And with good reason. American newscasting in Europe was still an ad hoc proposition that depended on borrowed radio facilities controlled by sometimes-uncooperative bureaucracies. Furthermore, because direct news reportage from Europe was still an infrequent feature of CBS programming, the network had no European reporters of its own and instead was in the habit of recruiting them on an as-needed basis from among newspaper correspondents. To procure both broadcasting facilities and newscasters in five different cities hundreds of miles apart from each other, and then to meld these components into a smooth round-robin of commentary, an eight-hour lead time hardly seemed sufficient.

Nevertheless, with the exception of

Rome, where they failed to obtain broadcast facilities, Murrow and Shirer somehow managed it with even a few moments to spare. At 8:00 P.M. (EST) on Sunday, March 13, 1938, Americans began hearing a succession of on-the-spot reports from Paris, London, Vienna, and Berlin on Europe's response to the *Anschluss*. The success of this experiment in multihookup overseas newscasting marked a new level of sophistication in radio journalism. Before long, radio listeners of the United States would be regarding international roundups as a commonplace of their news-consuming life.

But CBS's *Anschluss* coverage was momentous in another respect as well. In making final arrangements for the roundup's Vienna segment, Murrow had, in the interest of time, cut a corner. Rather than expend energy, sorely needed elsewhere, in chasing down a print journalist to make the Vienna broadcast, he decided to do it himself. As far as anyone can tell, that decision had been taken strictly because it seemed expedient and not because, during his time as a programming manager, Murrow had developed an ardent longing to try his hand at the microphone. Whatever the reason, it was a decision fraught with significance, and as the words "This is Edward Murrow speaking from Vienna" sped their way westward across the Atlantic, they signaled the arrival of a new and unusually luminous star in America's newscasting firmament.[3] Murrow's newscasting debut revealed a talent for spoken journalism that would soon make him

the most respected radio journalist in America.

Among the first to recognize the magnitude of this talent were Murrow's bosses in New York, who lost little time in exploiting it. As Hitler's aggressions and saber-rattling threats edged Europe to the brink of World War II, Murrow was on hand to report them from London on an increasingly regular basis. By the time the war became reality in September 1939, the day was fast approaching when nearly all Americans would be familiar with his arrestingly rich voice, lean sentences, and artful pauses.

In an early article lauding Murrow's newscasting abilities, the writer at one point declared, "He has more influence

Ed Murrow at work in London. Unidentified photographer, not dated. Murrow Center, Fletcher School of Law and Diplomacy, Tufts University, Medford, Massachusetts

## ED MURROW REPORTS THE HORRORS OF THE GERMAN CONCENTRATION CAMP AT BUCHENWALD    APRIL 15, 1945

As I walked down to the end of the barracks, there was applause from the men too weak to get out of bed. It sounded like the hand clapping of babies; they were so weak. . . .

As we walked out into the courtyard, a man fell dead. Two others—they must have been over sixty—were crawling toward the latrine. I saw it but will not describe it. . . .

We went to the hospital; it was full. The doctor told me that two hundred had died the day before. I asked the cause of death; he shrugged and said, "Tuberculosis, starvation, fatigue, and there are many who have no desire to live. It is very difficult." Dr. Heller pulled back the blankets from a man's feet to show me how swollen they were. The man was dead. Most of the patients could not move. . . .

Professor Richer said perhaps I would care to see the small courtyard. I said yes. He turned and told the children to stay behind. As we walked across the square I noticed that the professor had a hole in his left shoe and a toe sticking out of the right one. He followed my eyes and said, "I regret that I am so little presentable, but what can one do?" At that point another Frenchman came up to announce that three of his fellow countrymen outside had killed three S.S. men and taken one prisoner. We proceeded to the small courtyard. The wall was about eight feet high; it adjoined what had been a stable or garage. We entered. It was floored with concrete. There were two rows of bodies stacked up like cordwood. They were thin and very white. Some of the bodies were terribly bruised, though there seemed to be little flesh to bruise. Some had been shot through the head, but they bled but little. All except two were naked. I tried to count them as best I could and arrived at the conclusion that all that was mortal of more than five hundred men and boys lay there in two neat piles.

There was a German trailer which must have contained another fifty, but it wasn't possible to count them. The clothing was piled in a heap against the wall. It appeared that most of the men and boys had died of starvation; they had not been executed. But the manner of death seemed unimportant. Murder had been done at Buchenwald. God alone knows how many men and boys have died there during the last twelve years. Thursday I was told that there were more than twenty thousand in the camp. There had been as many as sixty thousand. Where are they now?

As I left that camp, a Frenchman . . . came up to me and said, "You will write something about this, perhaps?" And he added, "To write about this you must have been here at least two years, and after that—you don't want to write any more."

I pray you to believe what I have said about Buchenwald. I have reported what I saw and heard, but only part of it. For most of it I have no words. Dead men are plentiful in war, but the living dead, more than twenty thousand of them in one camp. And the country round about was pleasing to the eye, and the Germans were well fed and well dressed. American trucks were rolling toward the rear filled with prisoners. Soon they would be eating American rations, as much for a meal as the men at Buchenwald received in four days.

If I've offended you by this rather mild account of Buchenwald, I'm not in the least sorry. . . .

than a shipful of newspapermen."[4] The assertion had some merit. In the course of covering the European phase of World War II from its outset to its close in 1945, Murrow did indeed seem on occasion to exert a sizable influence on his American audiences. The clearest demonstrations of that were his reports on the devastating German air blitz over England, which began in August 1940. There were many—among them Winston Churchill and Franklin Roosevelt—who believed that his coverage of the blitz was an important factor in convincing Americans that their country must ultimately become involved in the struggle against Hitler.

Yet another testament to Murrow's influence was the enormous respect that much of his work engendered among print journalists, who were often in the habit of regarding radio reporters as the decidedly inferior stepchildren of their profession. By war's end, no one would have dreamed of relegating Murrow to that lesser status. In fact, several of his wartime broadcasts—most notably his firsthand accounts of an Allied bombing mission over Germany and of the horrors of a German concentration camp—were deemed so fine that they were printed verbatim in many newspapers, and they are commonly ranked today among the journalistic classics of World War II.

In trying to pinpoint the primary reasons for Murrow's emergence as American radio's foremost wartime newscaster, one observer thought that the main source

Microphone used by Ed Murrow in his wartime broadcasts from London. Courtesy Frank Stanton

The telegram from Ed Murrow asking William Shirer to dine in Berlin, which led to Shirer's newscasting career. Estate of William L. Shirer

of his strength lay in an "ability to compress and condense" the content of his reportage "without distorting" it.[5] For others, Murrow's greatest asset was a voice that invested whatever he said with an oracle-like authority. And for yet others, it was not so much Murrow's voice per se as it was the cadence of his delivery, which often seemed to enlarge the meaning of his words.

But perhaps Murrow's most important attribute—and the one radio audiences most appreciated—was his knack for pictorializing the news. In a report on American soldiers stationed in England, for example, he told his listeners: *In a showroom here in London there's a Rolls Royce engine with the side cut away. Any time during the day you can see a bunch of GIs standing around discussing it. The length of the piston stroke and the way the valve tappets work. It fascinates them. Most other Allied troops pass it by with scarcely a glance.*[6] The immediate purpose of this quick verbal depiction of a scene in wartime London was to underscore Murrow's observation that one of the things setting American soldiers apart from their Allied brothers in arms was their unabating fascination with modern technology. But the sketch also underscored what may have been Murrow's greatest strength—an eye for the offbeat vignette that imbued his broadcasts with vivid particularity.

## WILLIAM L. SHIRER
1904–1993

In the summer of 1937, after some twelve years of earning his living as a foreign correspondent for a succession of American newspapers and wire services, William Shirer was in trouble. At the moment, he was in Berlin, where since 1934 he had been working for the Hearst newspapers' Universal Service. But thanks to its failure to turn a profit of late, Universal was closing down, and Shirer's efforts to line up another correspondent's job were proving unsuccessful. For awhile Shirer remained calmly optimistic that some job would eventually turn up. And indeed one did, at the Berlin office of International News Service. But soon after settling into this new position, he was told that International was cutting back on its staff and that he was about to be let go, with two weeks' notice. As a result, by late August panic was setting in, and Shirer was beginning to have nightmare visions of being stranded in Europe with no means of supporting himself and his wife. Compounding the grimness of those visions was the fact that his wife was expecting the birth of their first child.

In the midst of this mounting anxiety, Shirer received a telegram from London that, although he did not yet know it, offered the lifeline he had been grasping for. It came from CBS's director of European programming, Ed Murrow, and its one-

Shirer (*center*) reviews a program script with two of his troublesome German censors.

Unidentified photographer, circa 1940. Estate of William L. Shirer

William Shirer broadcasts on the Munich crisis from a Berlin train station, September 20, 1938. The broadcast was to consist of interviews with other reporters about to catch a train for Godesburg, where a conference between Hitler and British Prime Minister Neville Chamberlain was to be held. But it got off to a shaky start when Shirer had to begin before any of his interviewees had shown up at the station. Nevertheless, it went well in the end, and CBS cabled him that the program had been "a knockout." Unidentified photographer, 1938. Estate of William L. Shirer

line message was an invitation to have dinner with Murrow at the Hotel Adlon in Berlin.

Beyond a free meal and some pleasant conversation at one of the German capital's finest hotels, Shirer did not expect much of this encounter. Most likely, he conjectured, Murrow was coming to Berlin on an information-gathering mission and simply thought that Shirer, well-seasoned observer of European affairs that he was, might have some useful leads on how to go about improving CBS's European programming. To Shirer's surprise, however, Murrow wanted more than just

leads; he wanted to offer Shirer a job. By evening's end, the two men had agreed that, assuming a positive reaction to the proposition at CBS headquarters in New York, Shirer would soon be assisting Murrow in arranging the network's European broadcasts.

Like Murrow, Shirer joined CBS's European operations as a behind-the-scenes facilitator. But also like Murrow, the network's hastily improvised *Anschluss* news roundup in March 1938 marked his debut as a newscaster. By the time all-out war came to Europe in 1939, Shirer had become a full-fledged radio journalist and

This photograph of Shirer marks the biggest scoop of his newscaster's career in the Third Reich. Seated at his typewriter in Compeigne, France, Shirer was preparing background notes for his on-site report of the French surrender to the Germans in June 1940. His radiocast on the event reached the United States some four or five hours before any other journalist managed to file a story on it, and because there was no corroboration from other sources, some momentarily questioned Shirer's veracity. Unidentified photographer. Estate of William L. Shirer

his reports were a regular feature of CBS's European news coverage.

When Shirer first joined CBS, he had been headquartered in Vienna. But by the late summer of 1939, his base was Berlin. Thus, as he set about the task of reporting the opening stages of World War II, he found himself plying his trade in a setting that was at best a mixed blessing. On the one hand, being in Berlin placed him at the center of Germany's Nazi regime and on many occasions afforded him access to information about its quest for the domination of Europe that could be obtained nowhere else. But thanks to the indifference of Hitler's Third Reich to such niceties as freedom of the press, having a bird's-eye view of much of Germany's war-making activities often counted for nothing, and as the war progressed through its first year, Shirer's ability to report the latest news was increasingly hampered by Nazi censorship. By September 1940, no fewer than three censors—one from Germany's propaganda ministry, another from its military establishment, and yet another from its foreign office—had to approve his news reports before they could be broadcast. On more than one occasion, his battles with this trio of deletion-prone officials resulted in his not going on the air at all. On September 9, for example, Shirer reported in his diary: "The three censors fought with me so long over the script of my two P.M. broadcast . . . that by the time they okayed it, there was not time for me to go on the air."[7]

In some cases, the constraints placed on Shirer by German censorship took the form of wholesale silencings. When it came, for instance, to such matters as a noticeable weakening in the German-Soviet alliance in the fall of 1940 and signs that Germany might be planning an invasion of the Soviet Union, Shirer was strictly forbidden to utter a word. But there were other occasions when the censorship amounted to little more than nit-picking. Thus, when Germany launched its attack on Holland and Belgium in May 1940, his censors, anxious to put the best face possible on this blatant act of aggression, insisted that Shirer refrain, in the lead sentence of his broadcast, from characterizing it as an "invasion."[8] After some argument, Shirer acquiesced, confident that despite the slightly more ambiguous rephrasing settled upon, his American listeners would know an invasion when they heard about it.

Despite the censors, Shirer's journalistic instincts for getting a good and truthful story were not entirely stifled. For although his censors carefully scrutinized every word of his broadcast scripts, their limited understanding of spoken American English sometimes left them unable to spot passages that ran contrary to the official Nazi propaganda line. As a result, Shirer often managed, through a combination of colloquial phrasing and an ironic tone in his voice, to make points in his broadcasts that his censors would have quickly excised, had they known what he was up to. At times he also found that he could get his message across by quoting directly from approved Nazi sources, such as Hitler's own public utterances or reports on the war found in Germany's tightly controlled newspapers. Because these sources were so patently propagandistic in their attempts to justify the German cause, he knew that his American audience would not take his citations at their face value and would realize that their real meaning lay somewhere between the lines.

Unfortunately, reports began reaching Berlin from German agents in the United States that Shirer was "getting by with murder."[9] As a result, by the fall of 1940, a team of new censors had been assigned to him who were considerably more adroit in thwarting his various ploys to evade them, and the day was fast approaching, Shirer feared, when his ability to report the news from Berlin in an objective manner would be nil.

Tighter censorship, however, was not the only thing bothering Shirer in the fall of 1940. In fact, it may have been the least of his problems. For his attempts to foil his Nazi censors had led to suspicions in the Third Reich that he was considerably more than a troublesome reporter who sometimes balked at parroting the Nazi interpretation of the current war news. At first, Shirer had only vague indications that something like this might be the case. But in late October, it was confirmed when a woman friend, who worked for German radio and was not particularly sympathetic to her country's Nazi regime, told him that she had seen documents suggesting that Shirer was encoding messages into his broadcasts that disclosed some of Germany's more closely held military secrets.

Shirer knew, of course, that there were no grounds for such an allegation. Nevertheless, he had seen enough of Hitler's regime to realize that, should it become intent on prosecuting him as an undercover agent, the want of hard evidence would not deter it from doing so. Consequently, Shirer decided that his newscasting days in the Third Reich were ended. In early December 1940, he was on his way back to the United States.

But Shirer's efforts to enlighten the American public on conditions in Germany were not over. During his years in Germany, first as a print journalist for Universal Service and then as a CBS newscaster, he had kept a private running commentary on the country's Nazi regime. In it he had recorded his impressions of conditions and events with a candor that Nazi censorship so frequently stifled in his reportage. To a large extent, keeping this diary was Shirer's way of assuaging the mixture of guilt and frustration that came with knowing that his German censors were routinely forcing him to compromise his professional standards for journalistic

honesty. Ultimately, however, this diary account proved to be considerably more than a personal vehicle for easing day-to-day emotional strains. Soon after returning to the United States, Shirer began arranging for its publication, and in the spring of 1941, his *Berlin Diary* was making its appearance in bookstores across America. At last Shirer had his chance to report the foibles, oppressions, and brutalities of Nazi Germany with a frankness that had long been denied him. *Time* characterized the book as "the most complete report yet to come out of wartime Germany," a judgment that was echoed in scores of other publications.[10] After so many years of feeling depressed and guilty about his inability to give the straight story, such praise must have struck him as sweet vindication indeed.

# 7

# ARTISTS AS FIELD CORRESPONDENTS

On the cover of its issue of December 27, 1943, *Life* magazine featured a painting by its artist-war correspondent Fletcher Martin, depicting a nurse ministering to the needs of a heavily bandaged American soldier wounded in the Allied campaign to drive the Germans from North Africa. Set against a nighttime backdrop that showed the bombed-out ruins of a Christian church in the distance, the picture had doubtless been chosen for *Life*'s cover because its good Samaritan tranquillity struck a note that seemed appropriate to the current wartime Christmas season. Martin's cover painting, however, was only a foretaste of what that issue of *Life* had in store for its readers: Inside was a full-color sequence of pictures, running continuously for thirty-two pages, portraying scenes of World War II. The work of six artists—four of whom were in the pay of *Life* and two of whom were officers in the navy—the pictures included war-related subject matter that spanned the globe. From the Pacific, there was Aaron Bohrod's painted record of the taking of a Japanese-occupied island named Rendova. Also from that part of the world were the renderings by Paul Sample, who had undertaken to paint crew life on a submarine sent out to patrol the seas for Japanese warships, and pictures from the hand of navy Lieutenant Dwight Shepler, showing some of the dramatic moments of the Battle of Guadalcanal. Also reproduced in the section were the paintings of Floyd Davis who, while stationed as an artist-correspondent in England, had had the chance to observe and draw the drama of the European air war. Finally, there were Fletcher Martin's depictions of the war in North Africa and navy Lieutenant Mitchell Jamieson's portrayal of phases of the Allied landings in Sicily.

The notion of enlisting trained artists to depict the scenes of war was not a new one. As a matter of fact, the impulse to record in visual form both the pains and glories of battle was as old as war itself. For centuries, however, the pictorialization of battles generally took place well after the fact. Moreover, it was often the work of artists who had not actu- ally witnessed the conflict they portrayed and who, in the pursuance of their aesthetic con- cerns, had little compunction about distorting the real facts of the event.

By contrast, the war paintings reproduced in *Life* in late 1943 represented an effort to portray war from firsthand observation, thereby creating pictures that offered authentic vignettes of the conflict. As such they were part of a tradition in battle art that was of a relatively recent vintage. It was not until the nineteenth century that revolutions in publish- ing gave birth to a widely disseminated illustrated press, which had, in turn, spawned the idea of the artist as a potential war correspondent. Thus, while *Life*'s artists could trace the roots of their endeavors back to time immemorial, the on-the-scene immediacy and authenticity of their paintings belonged to a school of wartime art that had its origin in the pictorial field reporting done by such artists as Constantin Guys during the Crimean War for the *London Illustrated News* and Winslow Homer during the Civil War for *Harper's Weekly*.

Since the likes of Guys and Homer had set out to draw their respective wars back in the mid-nineteenth century, some landmark changes in pictorial news reporting had oc- curred, which in many respects made the efforts of *Life*'s artists seem archaic and super- fluous in 1943. After all, one might well have asked, in the face of the legions of movie- newsreel makers and photographers covering World War II, why would anyone deem it desirable—much less necessary—to send artists out on much the same mission? What could they do with their pencils, brushes, and paints that the present state-of-the-art cam- eras could not do? Indeed, wasn't the mechanically derived visual image bound to docu- ment the war more accurately than one drawn freehand?

Questions along these lines did indeed arise, and in certain important quarters the answers to them did not run in favor of the field artists. The most notable case in point occurred in Congress in mid-June of 1943. At the moment the Appropriations Committee in the House of Representatives was reviewing the army's budget requests for fiscal year 1943–1944, which came to a total of 71.5 billion dollars. The figure seemed staggeringly large when measured against the substantially smaller military allocations of only a few years earlier, but with the country at war on two fronts, the committee's members were inclined to approve the funding with few questions asked. When it came, however, to an item in the proposed budget with a price tag on it of $125,000, the lawmakers' eyebrows were suddenly raised in disapproval. Several months earlier the army had organized a unit consisting of nineteen civilian and twenty-three uniformed artists who were delegated with the mission of recording the war in pictures, and the army had seen fit to earmark this relatively modest amount of taxpayer dollars for that venture. In doing so, it had not reck- oned with the House Appropriations Committee. With Alabama Congressman Joe Starnes

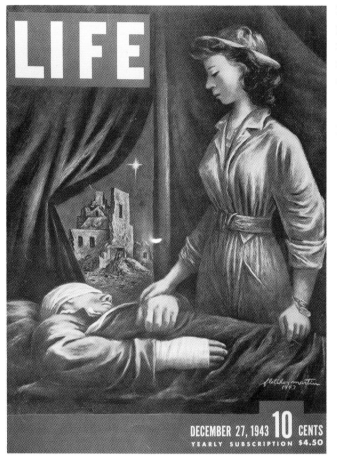

Field artist Fletcher Martin's painting of a nurse ministering to a soldier in North Africa as it appeared on the cover of *Life*, December 27, 1943. Fletcher Martin (1904–1979), 1943. © Time Warner Inc.

leading the attack and labeling the army's art project a "piece of foolishness" that the country could well live without, the committee quickly voted to strike the art allocation from the budget.[1]

When the army budget hearings were over, Starnes proudly declared of the committee's willingness to approve almost in toto the army's proposed budget: "We must not slacken the quickening pace, or the ever-increasing force of our blows."[2] But in light of what his committee had just done to the army's art program, he might have followed up that statement with a variant on a famous rallying cry from America's distant past. Echoing "millions for defense, but not one cent for tribute"—the country's rejoinder in 1797 to the demand of French officials for a payoff before negotiating American grievances against their country—Starnes could have ended his outburst of high-minded patriotism with "billions for defense, but not one cent for art!"

Although the cause of the field artists fared badly in Congress, there were others who believed in it. Chief among them were the editors at *Life* who, even before Pearl Harbor, had enlisted artists to record this country's escalating preparations for war and its naval involvement in convoying supplies to beleaguered Great Britain under the Anglo-American lend-lease agreements. The magazine's prodigious success, since its founding in the mid-1930s, rested almost entirely on its lively photographic picture stories. Nevertheless, it saw considerable value in the painted or drawn reportorial image. When Congress forced the army to disestablish its combat artists section in the summer of 1943, *Life* promptly took steps to hire most of the civilians who had joined the unit and saw to it that they were duly accredited as combat correspondents. By the late summer of 1943, the magazine had more than twenty field artists scattered around the world in its employ. At the same time, it opened its pages to painted and drawn portrayals of various military operations by navy and marine artists who, unlike their army counterparts, had escaped a congressional budget axing because their art endeavors represented only a secondary part of their assigned military duties.

Although such actions left no doubt of *Life*'s belief in the value of the combat artists, the texts that accompanied the magazine's many spreads featuring pictures done by its artists never offered much of an answer to the argument that modern photography made the combat artist's work largely unnecessary. One of the artists whom *Life* hired from the army's ill-fated art project, however, did attempt to answer that assertion. Ruminating over the problem in his wartime diary in the summer of 1943, he suggested that, whereas the mechanically produced photograph could state the objective facts of combat, it remained for the artist to infuse them with a "philosophic *point de départ*" and an "inner illumination."[3] In other words, whereas photographs of war had the edge in matters of physical accuracy, the combat artist could offer the viewer, through subjective expressions of color and composition, a sense of the human feelings—albeit of only one individual—engendered by its horrors and devastations.

## GEORGE BIDDLE

1885–1973

The author of that observation was George Biddle, a fifty-eight-year-old veteran of World War I, who at the moment was with American forces in North Africa. One of the artists that *Life* recruited from the army's short-lived art unit, Biddle was, in addition to being a painter of note, some-thing of a mover and shaker. Given the facts that he came from a socially well-connected Philadelphia family, was the brother of the present attorney general of the United States, and had been on a first-name basis with President Franklin Roosevelt ever since their school days together at Groton and Harvard, his moving and shaking often worked to good effect in certain high quarters. In the early days of the New Deal, for example, Biddle con-

This photograph of George Biddle sketching in North Africa in 1943 was taken by George Silk, a New Zealander who had just joined *Life*'s staff of war photographers. George Silk (born 1916) for *Life* magazine. © Time Warner Inc.

Biddle encountered this contorted corpse of a German soldier in Sicily. The dead youth, he noted, "lay pitched on his back, in one of those curiously surrealistic, Russian ballet-dancer poses, characteristic of the slain in battle. . . . His cheeks were shrunken. His long yellow hair was meticulously brushed. . . . By his open hand lay a pocket comb, half protruding from the case." George Biddle, 1943. Pen and ink on paper, 19.1 x 24.1 cm (7½ x 9½ in.). Michael Biddle

cluded that his old friend Roosevelt, while losing no time in launching measures to ease the sufferings of the current depression in general, was not giving enough consideration to possibilities for aiding some of the nation's hard-pressed artists. His own answer to the difficult plight of so many members of his profession was federal sponsorship of public art programs. When he outlined his proposal for the President in a "Dear Franklin" letter of May 1933, Roosevelt answered with a suggestion that Biddle come to Washington to discuss the matter further with various New Dealers. Among the eventual results of that interchange between the two "Grotties" was the establishment of the Federal Art Project under the Works Progress Administration.

Returning from Brazil late in 1942,

where he and his wife, sculptor Helene Sardeau, had just finished a collaborative commission for Rio de Janeiro's National Library, Biddle began to feel an itch to exert his influence yet again. Long past the age when he could serve his country in a military capacity, he nevertheless wanted to make a contribution to the current war effort. So, in January 1943, he was in Washington, utilizing his connections in the hope of finding a useful function for himself in the war. It was not long before his search turned something up. Armed with a memorandum given him by a general, expressing the army's desire to organize a group of field artists for recording the war, he was soon in the office of the assistant secretary of war, John McCloy, discussing with him the prospects for realizing such an enterprise. McCloy liked the idea. Within weeks, Biddle had become chairman of the War Department Art Advisory Committee and was hard at work recruiting artists. By late April, the organizational tasks were largely done. With nineteen civilian and twenty-three army artists now enlisted in the venture, Biddle was packing up enough drawing and painting supplies to last him six months and preparing to join American forces in North Africa, where he would begin his own career as a pictorial chronicler of war.

As was his habit throughout most of his life, Biddle kept a diary of his days as a field artist, where he noted, in often surprising detail, what he saw, how he worked, and his reactions to the events around him. On September 1, 1943, hav-

ing accompanied the final Allied drive to push the Germans from North Africa, he was now witnessing the Allied advance into Italy. He had seen enough of the war to know well the unspeakable miseries that it visited on civilians and soldiers alike. Doubtless it was with those miseries in mind that he brooded, in his diary that day, over the great discrepancy between the realities of this total war and the

"sugar-coated" images of it that were being fed to civilians back in the States.

In particular, he lamented the types of photographs that the Army Signal Corps was producing in its effort to record the war both for posterity and for distribution to the press at home. Thanks to military censorship's low tolerance for any "horror stuff," the Signal Corps photographers, he claimed, had given up on recording the

In this portrayal of a surrendering German in Italy, Biddle invested the scene with a nightmarish desolation that verged on the surreal. George Biddle, 1944. Oil on canvas, 101.6 x 127 cm (40 x 50 in.). United States Army Center of Military History, Washington, D.C.

In this painting, Biddle records some of the bodies of the many Italian civilians who had been killed during the Allied drive to occupy Naples in the fall of 1943. Some had fallen victim to Allied bombing, others to Axis sniping. Biddle based the picture on drawings made in a Neapolitan hospital whose corridors, he noted in his diary, were filled to overflowing with corpses. George Biddle, 1944. Oil on canvas, 40.6 x 50.8 cm (16 x 20 in.). Michael Biddle

Biddle came upon this advance group of British gunners on September 30, 1943, at a town just south of Naples. While making drawings of these soldiers, the shelling from a German howitzer forced him periodically to drop what he was doing and seek cover. "It is amazing," Biddle later observed, "how fast and accurately one can dive and how one can flatten out, when properly conditioned by the whine of a shell." George Biddle, 1943. Pen and ink on paper, 22.9 x 30.5 cm (9 x 12 in.). United States Army Center of Military History, Washington, D.C.

Even in defeat, Biddle found, German army officers remained arrogant and conceited, and it was that relentless sense of superiority that he sought to capture in this portrayal of two German officers who had been taken prisoner in North Africa. George Biddle, 1943. Oil on canvas, 25.4 x 35.6 cm (10 x 14 in.). United States Army Center of Military History, Washington, D.C.

less pleasant realities of war and were concentrating instead on taking pictures that put a decidedly bright face on things. As a result, their favorite subject matter had become such events as "major generals inspecting field bakeries with congressmen" and "doughboys feeding chocolates to Sicilian relatives." At least as far as Signal Corps photography was concerned, Biddle thus feared that the home front was being served up with a wartime imagery that amounted to little more than a "Charles Dana Gibson girl, waving an American flag."[4]

Biddle was determined that his own pictorial record of the war should not fall into that pattern of sunny, upbeat imagery. To be sure, during his eight months in Africa and Italy, he produced his share of drawings that could be categorized as pre- and post-battle local color—exotically garbed Algerian natives in a marketplace, for example, and officers and enlisted men at rest. Nevertheless, his main preoccupation lay ultimately with capturing scenes that were emblematic of the horrible waste of the conflict he had been sent to cover. War "spells frustration, destruction, fatigue, misery, despair," he wrote after returning home. "It is *Alice in Wonderland,* played in a madhouse."[5] It was that sense of gruesome insanity that informed so much of his wartime work.

In achieving his pictorial objectives, Biddle—despite his fifty-eight years—did not hang back from the rigors of the front. In the fall of 1943, he spent more than a month with the undersupplied

Third Infantry Division as it was working its way up the Italian peninsula, against stiff German opposition through unremitting rain and mud. His willingness to suffer the discomforts and hazards of this operation, which was strictly optional for him as a noncombatant, astonished his fighting companions. At one point in his diary, he noted that "they tell me that I am a little crazy."[6]

Periodically Biddle must have secretly agreed with that judgment, for there were times when the human devastation around him proved so difficult to bear that he momentarily could not bring himself to do the job that he was there to do. "There is a great deal of material to sketch about me in the quarry," his diary noted on one such occasion. "But somehow I can't do it. It is not just because I have been up all night in the cold, climbed a mountain carrying a 30-pound pack, and waded a river. . . . Under some circumstances reportage becomes, if not an act of sacrilege, at any rate a breach of taste."[7] Ultimately, however, Biddle accomplished his goals as a war chronicler, and in his renderings of the mangled bodies of dead soldiers, of homeless starving civilians left in war's wake, and of the bleak, defoliated, shell-holed landscapes, he did indeed offer a sobering glimpse into the war's tragic desolations.

## TOM LEA
BORN 1907

In the early spring of 1941, there were still some Americans—though diminishing rapidly in number—who held onto the hope that their country could avoid active involvement in World War II. The editors at *Life,* however, were not among them, and one of their current preoccupations was the production of a series of picture stories on the American military's escalating programs to prepare itself for the almost certain prospect of all-out war with the Axis powers.

One of those stories was on the army cavalry, and in planning its coverage of that soon-to-be-outmoded branch of the service, the magazine dispatched a letter to a young artist in El Paso, Texas, named Tom Lea, asking him for an illustration depicting a typical member of the First Cavalry Division at Fort Bliss. Just beginning to win a reputation as a capable illustrator, Lea readily obliged and thereby began his career as *Life*'s most prolific and widely traveled war artist. The magazine never ran his cavalry picture. Nevertheless, it liked his work well enough to commission pictures from him of other war-related subjects. By the late fall of 1941, having done four portraits of military trainees for a spread in one of the magazine's summer issues, Lea was in Newport, Rhode Island, boarding an American warship headed for the North Atlantic. On this occasion, his assignment from *Life*

Artist correspondent Tom Lea with the Seventh Marine Regiment on Peleliu. Unidentified photographer, 1944. Private collection

*Life*'s caption for Lea's portrayal of a battle-weary soldier read, "He left the States 31 months ago. He was wounded in his first campaign. . . . He half-sleeps at night and gouges Japs out of holes all day. Two thirds of his company has been killed or wounded. . . . How much can a human being endure?" Tom Lea, 1944. Oil on canvas, 91.4 x 71.1 cm (36 x 28 in.). United States Army Center of Military History, Washington, D.C.

was to produce a pictorial record of the navy's efforts to protect the convoys carrying much-needed supplies to war-torn Britain against German U-boat attacks. It was while covering this unofficial American war against Germany that Lea heard that the Japanese had attacked Pearl Harbor and that his country was now formally at war with both Germany and Japan.

Over the next two years, Lea traveled widely for *Life.* For more than sixty days, beginning in mid-August 1942, he lived aboard the naval carrier *Hornet,* and in

that period he produced a comprehensive chronicle of that ship's role in Allied operations in the South Pacific. Leaving the *Hornet* only a few days before its sinking at the Battle of Santa Cruz, he went to China the following year and there produced a number of striking portraits of wartime notables, among them Chiang Kai-shek and General Claire Chennault.

Lea's work on the *Hornet* and in China was only a mild preamble to what proved to be his most formidable wartime assignment. On a morning in mid-September 1944, having attached himself to Marine forces in the Pacific, Lea was on a naval transport preparing to join the invasion of Peleliu in the Palau Islands west of the Philippines.

The taking of this island containing a Japanese airstrip, Marine division commander Major General William Rupertus had predicted, would be "rough but fast."[8] He was only half right. The battle for Peleliu was indeed rough, but it was by no means fast. Facing a substantial contingent of Japanese forces securely fortified and amply supplied in a network of concrete pillboxes, tunnels, and natural caves, the Americans did not succeed in eliminating the last vestiges of their opposition until six weeks after their initial landing. By then, the casualty lists had mounted to more than 1,500 dead and more than 6,000 wounded. When all was over, the Battle of Peleliu had become one of the costliest Pacific island victories of the war. It was estimated that, for every Japanese soldier killed there, it had required the expendi-

ture on average of 1,589 rounds of heavy and light ammunition.

Going into Peleliu between the first and second invasion wave on September 15, Lea witnessed some of the heaviest fighting of this difficult operation, and practically from the moment he first hit the beach, it was clear that the drawing supplies he had brought with him were not going to see nearly as much use as he would have wished. Between the severe discomfort engendered by the island's 115-degree heat, the enemy's stiff resis-

tance, and the human suffering about him, attempts to record what he was seeing often proved difficult in the extreme. The most Lea could manage during much of his stay on Peleliu was to file away the events passing before him in his visual memory, and only after he was safely back on a ship was he able to begin recording the struggle for Peleliu in its early stages.

In the end, however, that was quite good enough. Basing his finished work mostly on hasty sketches drawn on shipboard while the memories of his day and a half

The inspiration for this painting came as its maker, Tom Lea, was moving toward Peleliu in a landing craft. "Over the gunwale of a craft abreast of us," the artist recalled, "I saw a marine, his face painted for the jungle, his eyes set for the beach, his mouth set for murder." Tom Lea, 1944. Oil on canvas, 55.9 x 106.7 cm (22 x 42 in.). United States Army Center of Military History, Washington, D.C.

This portrayal of an American soldier meeting his death on the beaches of Peleliu was Tom Lea's frankest commentary on the human cost of war, and when *Life* published it, a number of readers took offense at its gory harshness. But other readers thought that the picture offered a much-needed dose of reality. Tom Lea, 1944. Oil on canvas, 92.7 x 71.1 cm (36½ x 28 in.). United States Army Center of Military History, Washington, D.C.

on Peleliu were still fresh, Lea ultimately produced a painted chronicle that offered some of the most vivid glimpses into the Pacific war.

Among the most memorable was his rendering of a Marine as he stood glaring over the gunwale of his landing craft toward the beach in a state of almost hypnotized determination. That picture eventually became the pictorial symbol of Peleliu, but several other of Lea's pictures might have served that purpose as well. One titled *Two-Thousand-Yard Stare* was the portrait of a seasoned veteran with no apparent wounds as he wandered dazedly in a sick bay temporarily established in a shell hole. The subject had weathered the Pacific war for thirty-one months, but Peleliu had posed a test of his mettle that was beyond endurance. He stood there, Lea later wrote, "staring stiffly at nothing. His mind had crumbled . . . his jaw hung, and his eyes were like two black empty holes in his head."[9] Yet another of Lea's most arresting pictures from Peleliu was *The Price.* When it appeared in *Life,* the work drew indignant shudders from several readers, and understandably so. Based on what Lea saw as he himself was struggling for cover against enemy shelling in his first moments on the beach, the picture showed a soldier, an arm and half his face in bloody shreds, stumbling onto the sand to his death.

Lea completed his Peleliu paintings at his home in El Paso, Texas. But the devastations of what he had seen in the Pacific had taken their toll on him. "I felt I had no real right to be home," he later wrote, and he kept wondering why he had come through Peleliu safely when so many others had not.[10] The finishing of the Peleliu series thus became something more than a matter of filling his correspondent's obligations to *Life.* Feeling that he would never truly be "back home" until these pictures were done, he regarded his work on them as a guilt-relieving catharsis.

## DAVID FREDENTHAL
### 1914–1958

Of all the artists who joined the army art unit early in 1943 and became correspondents for *Life* following the unit's dissolution, none was better suited to the demands of portraying the action of war than David Fredenthal. For this Detroit-born artist, the spontaneous on-site pen drawing was as compulsive a habit as liquor is for the alcoholic. "I sketch unceasingly . . . everywhere I go," he once wrote, and it was said that he never went anywhere—even to a corner store for cigarettes—without three or four pens and a drawing pad tucked in his pocket.[11] Equally important was Fredenthal's genius for spotting the compositional richness of a subject and his ability to record the full texture of that richness in a matter of only

Photograph of David Fredenthal taken by *Life* photographer Alfred Eisenstaedt toward the end of the war. Alfred Eisenstaedt (born 1898) for *Life* magazine, circa 1945. © Time Warner Inc.

a few seconds. In short, the mesh between Fredenthal's skills and the tasks of a wartime field artist seemed almost perfect. If any human hand was capable of distilling the rapid movement and confusions of battle into meaningful pictures, it was his.

Fredenthal's first assignment as a field artist was in the Pacific, where he covered the military operations commanded by General Douglas MacArthur. In the several months spent there, he went along on three island invasions, the most memorable of which, for him at least, was the American beach landing at Arawe in New Britain in mid-December 1943.

The taking of Arawe struck some military planners, in retrospect, as strategically unnecessary in the struggle to drive the Japanese from the Southwest Pacific.

But although Arawe's military value might have been negligible, the painted and drawn record that Fredenthal made of its capture decidedly was not. Within that body of work, depicting the operation from its initial preparation stages to final landing, Fredenthal succeeded as few field artists did in pictorializing the tensions, fears, chaos, and pain that defined so much of the Pacific island fighting of World War II. If George Biddle had ever been asked to substantiate his assertion that the drawn or painted image was superior to the photograph when it came to recording the "feeling" of combat, he had only to point to Fredenthal's pictures from Arawe. Shortly after a selection of them appeared in *Life,* a reader wrote in that no pictures of the war—photographic or

This drawing from the battle for Arawe amply testifies to Fredenthal's remarkable facility for recording the sense of movement and tension inherent in combat. David Fredenthal, 1943. Pen and ink on paper, 14 x 21.6 cm (5½ x 8½ in.). Ruth Ann and Robinson Fredenthal. © Ruth Ann and Robinson Fredenthal

In this painting Fredenthal depicts American soldiers moving cautiously onto Arawe's
narrow beach, their eyes scanning the dense jungle ahead
of them for Japanese snipers
and bunkers. David Fredenthal, 1944. Watercolor on paper, 53.3 x 74.9 cm (21 x
29½ in.). United States
Army Center of Military History, Washington, D.C.

painted—had impressed her more than
these. "For a few dreadful moments," she
wrote, "I was there—clinging desperately
to a sinking rubber boat, hugging the
ground fearfully to escape strafing planes
. . . weeping from utter exhaustion!" But
perhaps the impact of the Arawe pictures
was best summed up by another field artist, Howard Cook, who upon seeing the
*Life* spread, declared that "the term artist-
war-reporter" was "too shallow a tag" for
Fredenthal.[12]

Fredenthal did not have much time to
revel in such accolades when *Life* published them in its letters-to-the-editor section early in September 1944. By then, he
was on his way to Europe to cover the Partisan war against German forces in Yugoslavia. This was a part of the European
conflict that was largely inaccessible to
American correspondents, and after arriving in Italy via passage arranged by *Life,*
Fredenthal had to fall back on his own ingenuity to complete the rest of his journey.
It was an ad hoc proposition at best. After
hitching a ride with a British commando
unit headed for a raid along Yugoslavia's
Dalmatian coast, he made his way to an
island, where a contingent of Partisans assisted him in getting to the Yugoslavian
mainland. There, drawing all the way, he
finally reached Belgrade in October, just
in time to witness the liberation of that
capital from German hands by a combination of Partisan and Russian forces.

Out of this adventure came a series of
sketches that, in their way, were every bit
as arresting as the work resulting from

This painting was a synthesis of two sights witnessed by Fredenthal on the beaches of Arawe—the body of a soldier (*left*) who had been killed just as he reached shore and another soldier huddled in post-battle exhaustion and crying softly to himself. David Fredenthal, 1944. Watercolor on paper, 53.3 x 74.9 cm (21 x 29½ in.). United States Army Center of Military History, Washington, D.C.

Fredenthal's Arawe experience. Whether the subject was a Russian soldier and his Partisan ally ducking enemy shells as they advanced through a field or a Belgrade mother greeting her Partisan son after three years of separation, his drawings needed no captions. In their emotionally charged spontaneity, they spoke for themselves. As one critic back in the United States later put it, this visual reportage from Eastern Europe finally put to rest the question of how to go about obtaining the best war art. The answer, he said, was simple: "Send Fredenthal."[13]

## BERNARD PERLIN
### BORN 1918

Many of *Life*'s field artists saw a good deal of combat during World War II and, in the course of doing their job, came in close contact with the hazards of battle. But of all the frontline experiences claimed by these visual chroniclers of the war, perhaps the most unusual belonged to Bernard Perlin. Hired by the Office of War Information to work on posters in its domestic section in 1942, Perlin had been let go from that organization the following year in the wake of a sharp congressional cutback in its funding. Shortly thereafter, *Life* took him on as one of its field artists, and in late 1943 he was headed for Africa, where the magazine had assigned him to cover war-related activity in Sudan and Eritrea, a former Italian colony that had fallen to the British in 1941.

Upon reaching Cairo en route, however, it became abundantly apparent to Perlin that nothing of any real import was happening at either of his two assigned destinations. As a result, he paid only a brief visit to Sudan and never bothered to go to Eritrea at all. Although apparently realizing that the assignment had been a mistake, *Life* seemed to feel no great urgency about shifting Perlin to a more newsworthy front. After failing to obtain Allied authorization for him to go to Italy, the magazine pretty much forgot about him, leaving him a correspondent without any immediate purpose.

This turn of events was not entirely without its compensations. A center of British operations in Africa and the Middle East, Cairo was a colorful city offering many pleasures, and for awhile Perlin did not find it particularly onerous to be left to his own devices there. Eventually, however, he began feeling guilty about his leisurely existence at *Life*'s expense, and after several months of tasting the sights and sounds of Cairo, his sense of guilt got

Photograph of Bernard Perlin taken shortly after returning to the United States from his Greek adventures. Jean Snow (lifedates unknown), 1944. Private collection

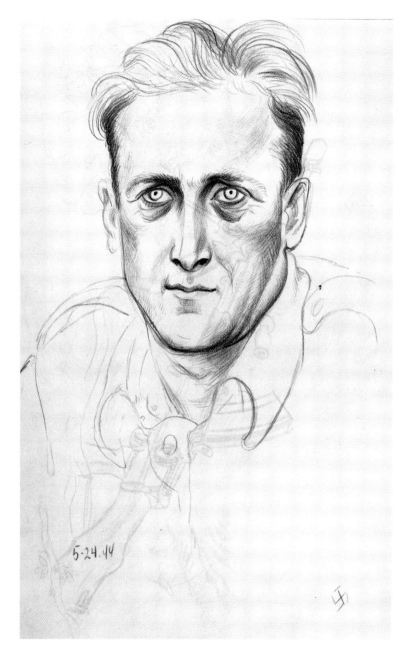

5-24.44

Among the sketches Perlin made on Samos was this portrait of the German soldier whom his party took pris-oner. Bernard Perlin, 1944. Pencil on paper, 34.9 x 21 cm (13¾ x 8¼ in.). Private collection

the best of him. The time had come, he decided, to begin behaving like a war cor-respondent, and if *Life* did not see fit to give him any definite new assignment, then perhaps he ought to devise one of his own.

And that is precisely what he did.

In late May 1944 Perlin was aboard a small craft in the Aegean Sea furtively making its way, under cover of night, to the German-occupied Greek island of Samos. With him were a British military observer and a small group of Greek sol-diers intent on attacking the German de-fenses there and, at the same time, plant-ing disinformation among the Germans regarding Allied strategies for the invasion of Europe. In meeting the first objective, the commandos were only minimally suc-cessful. They did, however, fulfill the sec-ond one, in a sequence of events that could have been scripted in Hollywood and that involved capturing a German and an Ital-ian soldier, filling them with misleading indications about Allied operations, and then intentionally letting them escape. But as this made-for-the-movies plot un-folded, it became fraught with more drama than the commandos or their field artist might have wished. The scheme's success hinged on allowing the German prisoners to escape in a situation where their flight would seem natural. Unfortu-nately, that situation came during an en-emy ambush that sent the commandos scattering for safety in all directions. In the confused panic, Perlin, along with two other members of the party, found refuge in a small cave, and for more than a day, the trio—one of them suffering from a broken arm—hovered there anxiously while German soldiers combed the nearby terrain for them and the rest of their companions.

Eventually the band of guerrillas managed to elude their German pursuers. After about a week on the island, spent largely moving from one hiding place to another, and several anxious nights of fruitless signaling for a rescue boat, they were finally picked up by a British patrol boat that took them to a base of British undercover operations in Turkey.

Perlin admitted many years later that his voluntary exposure to the perils of commando warfare on Samos, all in the name of obtaining a picture story for *Life,* seemed "pretty foolhardy." But at the time he reveled in it, and about a month after escaping from Samos, he was preparing to join a second commando expedition, this time onto the German-held Greek mainland. Expected to last some fifteen days, the mission consisted of eleven British soldiers, a Greek interpreter, and Perlin, and its purpose was to conduct forays against German installations and gather information from Greek Resistance fighters that might prove useful in planning the full-scale British liberation of Greece, which finally took place in the fall of 1944.

On landing at a village in the Peloponnesus, the twelve commandos and their field artist, according to Perlin, were greeted by local inhabitants as if they were

A pair of Greek Resistance fighters sketched by Perlin toward the end of his stay in Nazi-occupied Greece. Bernard Perlin, 1944. Pencil on paper, 42.5 x 32.7 cm (16¾ x 12⅞ in.). Private collection

In this picture, drawn from his experience on Samos, Perlin depicted himself and two of his comrades hovering in a cave while Germans, who had just ambushed their party, searched for them in the rocky terrain nearby. Against the chance that the Germans might find them, Perlin is seen here burning some papers that his companions did not want the enemy to find on them. Bernard Perlin, 1944. Gouache on paper, 33 x 50.8 cm (13 x 20 in.). United States Army Center of Military History, Washington, D.C.

Perlin depicts himself kneeling by the side of a peasant hut on Samos while one of his companions asks the young girl at the door for help in evading the Germans who were searching for them. As a correspondent, Perlin was forbidden to carry arms. But given the perilous situation, he decided to flout that rule and armed himself with a small pistol. Bernard Perlin, 1944. Gouache on paper, 27.9 x 41.9 cm (11 x 16½ in.). United States Army Center of Military History, Washington, D.C.

In this scene from his sortie into the German-occupied Peloponnesus, Perlin portrays the trek of his commando party down a mountainside following the wounding of one of the party's members. Bernard Perlin, 1944. Gouache on paper, 27.9 x 33 cm (11 x 13 in.). United States Army Center of Military History, Washington, D.C.

the whole British army come to free the area from the German yoke. Warm welcome or not, the mission was plagued with misfortunes practically from the outset. First, the radio that was meant to keep the commandos in touch with their home base in Turkey broke down. Then, while preparing a joint ambush with Resistance fighters on an approaching column of sixty German soldiers in a mountain village, a grenade in the commandos' own arsenal accidentally exploded, seriously wounding one of their party in the leg.

As it turned out, the German column never showed up. But the commandos did not have much time to dwell on their disappointment with missing the chance to take on the enemy. They now had a severely wounded comrade to care for, and as his condition worsened in the days that followed, the raiding party's preoccupation was to find medical treatment for him. Compounding the mission's troubles yet

further, the vessel that was to pick the raiders up for some reason never materialized at its appointed rendezvous. By the time a small British ship finally did appear to carry them away, the wounded soldier's leg, having developed gangrene, had been amputated, and the two-week foray into enemy territory had stretched into a month.

In terms of its original purposes, the mission was pretty much a total failure. For the young field artist who chronicled the adventure, however, it was quite another matter. Having begun his correspondent's career relegated to an unnewsworthy backwater, Perlin had managed something that few other reporters had: He became privy to one of the most secretive phases of the war's military operations, and the picture story that he derived from his initiation into the ways of commando warfare in Samos and the Peloponnesus was nothing less than a journalistic scoop.

## AARON BOHROD

1907–1992

At about the same time that George Biddle was departing for the Allied front in Africa, another member of the army's art unit, Aaron Bohrod, was preparing to make his way to the Pacific war. Trained at the Art Institute of Chicago and the Art Students League in New York City, this midwestern painter had barely settled into his recent appointment as artist-in-residence at Southern Illinois Normal University when he received his invitation to become a combat artist. His situation at Southern Illinois was a "happy one," Bohrod later recalled, that seemed to offer the best of all possible worlds.[14] While his light teaching responsibilities and open-house sessions at his studio left him ample time to pursue his own work, the give-and-take with students also moved him toward a better understanding of what he wanted to achieve in his painting. Comfortable and rewarding though his new position was, Bohrod viewed the offer from the army as an opportunity not to be missed. On the evening of April 22, 1943, amid the gloom of a wartime dimout, he boarded a Dutch steamship in San Francisco that was to carry him to his first Pacific stop, the American base at New Caledonia west of Australia.

New Caledonia was safely behind the current perimeters of Pacific combat, and after being confined to this French island colony for several weeks following his ar-

rival there, Bohrod became restless. He had used the time profitably, painting scenes of the tame military life there. But now he was ready to try his hand at what he understood to be the most important part of his job as a field artist. "If we don't get to do something that is definitely War," he impatiently noted in a diary account of his time in the Pacific, "our mission in my eyes . . . will be decidedly incomplete." That is not to say, however, that Bohrod was unqualifiedly enthusiastic over the prospect of jotting down sketches in the heat of enemy fire. When his complaints about being kept from the front lines of active combat were met with assurances that eventually he would "see plenty," he mused, "I'm not sure I want to see plenty. A little will do me fine."[15]

Finally in late June of 1943, the chance to blood himself came Bohrod's way. With an eye to driving the Japanese from their air base on Munda in the New Georgia island group, American forces were preparing an amphibious assault at Rendova, a small island off Munda. Along with two other field artists, Bohrod was invited to come along, and when asked whether he preferred to go in with the first or second wave of the invasion, he opted for the first, largely because, Bohrod said, he "feared to look afraid."[16]

Rendova proved to be one of those rare Pacific landing operations that went pretty much according to plan. Against only a modest amount of opposition from the Japanese, American forces gained control of the island in fairly short order and with

a minimum of casualties. As a result, though among the first to make his way from a landing barge onto a beach, Bohrod did not witness Pacific island fighting at its worst. Nevertheless, in the time he spent on Rendova, he did experience what it was like to face an enemy in the damp, hot, and densely forested jungles of the Pacific. He also discovered the hazards of ignoring warnings that he should stick close to his landing party. Setting out to get a sense of what was happening at another landing area, he eventually found himself totally isolated, mired in mud nearly up to his hips and feeling the panic that came with realizing that an unseen enemy could well be lurking in the surrounding trees. "The quiet was ominous," he wrote afterward. "I imagined a sniper in every tree. . . . I was scared to death, and tired, dead tired. . . . Huddling within myself to present as small a target as possible, I began to trudge along." Although this isolation from American forces in fact lasted only a short time, "it had seemed a year," he said.[17]

Bohrod's brush with a fairly full range of the physical discomforts and fears that were typically the lot of the combatant in Pacific island fighting may not have been happy in the actual experience, but it did pay a rather rich pictorial dividend. Working from a combination of memories, hasty field sketches, and photographs that he had taken, the artist ultimately produced, on his return to New Caledonia, a series of fifteen paintings documenting the Rendova operation.

Because Congress had disbanded the military art unit of which he was a part when he went to Rendova, Bohrod feared that the efforts expended on these pictures had gone for naught, and that his career as a combat artist was at an end. He was wrong on both counts. By the fall of 1943, having picked up his contract with the army, *Life* was preparing to feature the majority of Bohrod's Rendova paintings in its pages and arranging for their creator to cover the war in Europe.

Bohrod landed in England to carry out that new assignment in May 1944. On the surface, his arrival appeared to be perfectly timed. It was clear that the Allies were about to launch their long-expected cross-channel invasion somewhere on the coast of France, and Bohrod hoped that he would have a chance to portray this momentous event firsthand. There was one problem, however: The order had come down through the military hierarchy that only a limited number of the press would be allowed to accompany the operation in its opening phases, and a *Life* field artist was not deemed important enough to be included in that number. As a result, when the invasion of France's Normandy coast began on June 6, 1944, a much-dismayed Bohrod was left cooling his heels in London. Worse yet, the prospect of winning permission to join the invasion forces at some point in the near future seemed extremely dim.

But the long odds against Bohrod's getting to the Normandy beachhead began to shorten when he joined forces with an-

Contrary to the impression created by its backdrop, this picture of Aaron Bohrod, which appeared on the cover of *Life* on April 30, 1945, was not shot in some war-ravaged European town that the artist had visited. Rather, Bohrod posed for it long after he had returned from Europe, and the picture shows him seated among the debris of a building that was being torn down in Chicago. Myron Davis (born 1919) for *Life* magazine. © Time Warner Inc.

other *Life* artist, Byron Thomas. As anxious as Bohrod was to see the battle unfolding across the channel, Thomas was soon at work trying to finagle a means for getting himself and Bohrod to France, and on June 8 he had a stroke of luck: He stumbled across one Lieutenant Worthington, a press officer for the Merchant Marine, whose Liberty ships were charged with carrying men and supplies to Normandy. Worthington had not yet succeeded in finding a single correspondent interested in covering the role of the Merchant Marine in the invasion, and in the hope that Bohrod and Thomas might give some pictorial attention to it, he agreed to obtain a place for them on one of his service's Normandy-bound ships. He warned the two artists, however, that because they lacked proper authorizations, they probably would not be allowed to leave the vessel. Still, as far as Thomas and Bohrod were concerned, Worthington's offer was better than nothing. At least they would be within sight of the action. Besides, once they were that far, proper authorization or not, they just might find a way to finesse themselves onto the beach.

As it turned out, the finessing did not prove difficult. As Thomas noted later, the nearer a correspondent came to the front lines of battle, the less likely it was that a military official would insist on seeing his certified credentials. Thus, setting sail on their Liberty ship from an Allied staging area in the south of England on June 11, Thomas and Bohrod were by morning of the next day wading onto Normandy's Omaha Beach. Once there, with sketchbooks and cameras in hand, they immediately set about recording what they saw.

During his two days in Normandy, Bohrod did not see any active ground fighting, which by D-Day plus six had generally moved some distance from the landing beaches. But he did see a good deal of the massive, unceasing stream of arms and men that was being fed into the Normandy operation. One of the most striking pictures that Bohrod derived from his unauthorized channel crossing was a canvas depicting an unbroken line of soldiers, weighted down with their gear, trudging up a hill from Omaha Beach. Also among his pictorial records of Normandy was a painting indicating that Bohrod's experience at Rendova had not fully taught him the wisdom of not wandering off on his own in a war zone. The subject of the picture was the ruins of a Romanesque church at the French town of Colleville. When Bohrod happened upon this town on a solitary jaunt away from Omaha, the area around it still harbored German snipers. The artist, however, was not aware of that hazard at the time, and he did not learn of it until several days after his return to England, when the *London Times* reported that the Allies had only just secured Colleville.

Bohrod's portrayal of an assault group on Rendova. Aaron Bohrod, 1943. Gouache on board, 34.2 x 45.7 cm (13½ x 18 in.). United States Army Center of Military History, Washington, D.C.

Bohrod's portrayal of American troops inside Germany at the end of a day of fighting. Aaron Bohrod, 1945. Gouache on board, 40.6 x 61 cm (16 x 24 in.). United States Army Center of Military History, Washington, D.C.

The paintings and drawings produced by the artist-correspondents of World War II vary enormously in their approach to the subjects they depict. Some of these pictures show considerable concern for accuracy of detail; others are strictly impressionistic. Some emphasize action and movement; others focus on mood and emotion. It would be fair to say that if any two field artists had ever found themselves crouched, sketchbook in hand, on the same landing beach, the two resulting pictures would have been, more likely than not, quite different from each other. When George Biddle, as chairman of the army's War Art Unit, undertook in March 1943 to advise newly recruited members of that group on how to approach their tasks as war-chroniclers, he wrote, "You may be guided by Blake's mysticism, by Goya's cynicism and savagery, by Delacroix's romanticism, by Daumier's humanity and tenderness; or better still follow your own inevitable star."[18] In other words, there was no clear objective standard defining their mission, and it was entirely up to the individual artists to determine how to interpret the war. The result was that their respective portrayals of the war often became highly personalized distillations of what they saw, as reflective of their own emotional responses to war as they were depictions of actual occurrences.

But did that detract from the value of these artists' records of the war? If one were expecting their pictures to embody a litany of precise details about the war's events, then the answer to that question in many cases would be yes. But while sometimes short on visual exactitude, they were often long on atmosphere, and when it came to visually recording the textures of the war, they did indeed perform a useful reportorial function.

# WAR NEWS IN THE FUNNY PAPERS

## MILTON CANIFF'S *TERRY AND THE PIRATES*

"You've brought the war with Japan closer and clearer to me than all the movies, editorials, and radio commentators. You bring it to us in *all* its phases. . . . I sincerely think that in your line you're a genius." So wrote a woman from Chicago in the fall of 1944, and if one had to guess the object of this effusive praise, one would be inclined to think that it must have been directed to some veteran reporter in the Pacific with a special gift for vivid battle description. In fact, the recipient of this praise was not a news reporter at all. Nor was it someone who had ever even seen a Pacific battlefront. Rather it was Milton Caniff (1907–1988), creator of *Terry and the Pirates,* a syndicated comic strip whose lively array of characters had been fighting Japanese aggression in Asia since well before Pearl Harbor.

In putting his serialized story line on a wartime footing, Caniff was by no means unique. While the leading protagonists of his *Terry and the Pirates* raced from adventure to adventure, doing their level best to subdue the Japanese demons who had overrun the Asian Pacific, other comic-strip characters were also contributing to the war effort. In Ham Fisher's *Joe Palooka,* for example, the strip's heavyweight champion hero had forsaken the ring, joined the army, and was slogging his way with the Allies through the battlefronts of North Africa and Italy. Elsewhere, the pilot heroine of Russell Keaton and Glenn Chaffin's *Flying Jenny* was taking on

Self-portrait with the hero and villainess of his comic strip, *Steve Canyon.* Milton Caniff, 1947. Watercolor and pencil on paper, 49.1 x 48.6 cm (19⁵⁄₁₆ x 19⅛ in.). Cartoon, Graphic, and Photographic Research Library, The Ohio State University, Columbus. © Estate of Milton Caniff

Caniff's most talked-about *Terry and the Pirates* installment of the war, where Flip Corkin delivers a sermon to new army pilot Terry Lee. Cartoon, Graphic, and Photographic Research Library, The Ohio State University, Columbus. © Tribune Media Services, Inc.

the German Luftwaffe, and the detective in Norman Marsh's *Dan Dunn* was tracking down German saboteurs. Even Little Orphan Annie was doing her bit by uncovering abuses in civilian wartime rationing.

But although plots of many other strips focused on the war, none did it better or more convincingly than *Terry and the Pirates.* Indeed, a good many of the nation's funny-paper readers shared the Chicago lady's perception that Caniff's wartime fabrications were in their own peculiar fashion as authentic a news source on the war as the battlefront dispatches found on their daily newspaper's front page.

To some extent, the sense of realism in *Terry and the Pirates* rested on Caniff's rigid insistence on visual accuracy when it came to the accoutrements of war, and no plane, United States Army rifle, or Nazi dagger was drawn into his strip until he was absolutely sure of precisely how it looked. Also contributing to the strip's veracity was the fact that Caniff often modeled his characters on real people, the most memorable being ace army pilot "Flip Corkin," who looked and talked like Caniff's old college buddy and much-celebrated air hero, Colonel Philip Cochran. But perhaps the most engaging element of realism in *Terry and the Pirates* was the timely factuality that was so often woven into Caniff's plots. When, for example, the strip's title character, Terry Lee, embarked in 1943 on his training to become an army fighter pilot under the tutelage of Flip Corkin, Caniff went to great pains to ensure that the instructional episodes were an accurate mirror of the real thing. And apparently he succeeded. By the time Terry Lee had finished his training, at least one army air base had taken to posting clippings of Caniff's strip because

of the "sound advice" they contained for would-be flyers.

Occasionally *Terry and the Pirates* also appropriated the functions of the editorial page, and one observer claimed that when it came to rallying popular support for the war, Caniff's strip was one of the most potent forces around. The most memorable evidence of that was a strip that appeared in the fall of 1943, where Flip Corkin delivered a bit of a sermon on

Caniff's drawing of Lieutenant Colonel Flip Corkin, the character patterned on his old college friend, army flying ace Philip Cochran, who is pictured above. Milton Caniff, not dated. Watercolor and ink on board, 27 x 18.7 cm (10⅝ x 7⅜ in.). Cartoon, Graphic, and Photographic Research Library, The Ohio State University, Columbus. © Estate of Milton Caniff

the great debt that American combat pilots owed to their ground crews and the defense workers back home. The homily brought an avalanche of adoring letters to Caniff, and members of Congress thought so well of it that it was read into the *Congressional Record.*

# 8

# THE AFRICAN AMERICAN PRESS IN WARTIME

The black press's "Double V" campaign expressed itself not only in editorials and columns. It also was the inspiration for many celebrity news pictures. In this photograph, taken for the *Pittsburgh Courier,* two luminaries of the black community indicate their support for "Victory at Home and Abroad." On the left is boxer Harry Bobo, "Pittsburgh's idol of the roped arena"; on the right is Canada Lee, a boxer-turned-actor who had been a sensation in 1941 as the lead in Orson Welles's production of *Bigger Thomas.* Charles ("Teenie") Harris (born 1908), not dated. *Pittsburgh Courier* Photographic Archives

In August 1943, General George S. Patton paid a visit to a field hospital in Sicily with the intention of providing some morale-boosting comfort to soldiers who had been wounded in the recent Allied invasion of that island. Pausing at the bed of an unbandaged soldier with no apparent signs of a battle wound, Patton asked the patient what the source of his ills was. Suffering from battle fatigue, malaria, and chronic dysentery, the soldier simply replied, "I guess I can't take it." The words sent Patton into an uncontrollable rage. After cursing and slapping the man with his gloves, he stalked out of the hospital in a huff. Shortly thereafter, Patton visited yet another field hospital, where he again came upon a soldier suffering from battle fatigue. And again, Patton flew into a rage. Striking the man across the face and brandishing a pistol, the general exclaimed, "You are just a god-damned coward, you yellow son of a bitch. . . . You ought to be lined up against a wall and shot. In fact, I ought to shoot you myself."[1]

Today, such bullying and unfeeling behavior on the part of a prominent general would instantly rate front-page headlines in newspapers across the county. But in 1943, that did not happen. Although the journalists covering the Sicily campaign soon heard of these two unseemly occurrences, they readily acquiesced when General Dwight Eisenhower asked them to refrain from reporting the stories. As a result, the American public did not learn of the "slapping incidents" until some three months later, when Washington columnist Drew Pearson got wind of them through the journalists' grapevine and aired the story on his regular Sunday-evening broadcast.

Second only to the sheer outrageousness of Patton's behavior, perhaps the most remarkable aspect of this whole affair was the press's clear reluctance to report it. In the context of World War II, however, it was not so surprising that three months passed before this eminently sensational and newsworthy story should reach a journalist willing to report it. For strongly ingrained into the journalistic ethos of that conflict was a widespread conviction that the press had a patriotic obligation to avoid, whenever possible, taking a slant on the news that might erode civilian or military morale or reflect negatively on American institutions. Thus, although delayed reporting on the slapping incidents is easily the most dramatic example of journalistic self-restraint during World War II, on many occasions the press more or less voluntarily muzzled itself in the name of promoting the war effort.

In one quarter of the American journalistic establishment, however, this largely self-imposed restraint did not hold such strong sway. That quarter was the nation's African American press, and to explain its deviation from the wartime norm, one need go no further than the plight of its black readership.

On the eve of World War II, racial discrimination against blacks was, as it had always been, the single largest blemish on America's democratically based institutions. Denied the franchise in the South, the vast majority of African Americans were relegated to the most menial jobs everywhere. Routinely barred from parks, restaurants, hotels, theaters, and other public facilities, they faced severe discrimination in housing and all too often were the victims of mob brutalities that went unredressed in a justice system largely indifferent to their rights.

As a result, the African American press had always felt that its most important function was to take part in eliminating these inequities. And it was not prepared to sacrifice that function to some patriotic notion that calling attention to America's racial sins was potentially harmful to the country's cause. Quite to the contrary, if ever there was an appropriate time for publicizing those sins, it seemed to be now. With the war effort had come a tidal wave of morale-boosting democratic idealism, and amid all the high-minded rhetoric, this seemed to be the perfect moment to spotlight the fact that for American blacks that rhetoric had little basis in reality.

But while the black press did not intend to muffle its protests against racial injustice, it recognized an obligation to back the war effort. As a result, with the United States's entry into World War II in December 1941, the black press found itself grappling with the problem of striking a balance between its patriotic impulses to embrace the war effort and continuing its role as an outspoken critic of the country that effort was meant to defend. By mid-February 1942—thanks to the *Pittsburgh Courier,* one of the most widely circulated black newspapers in America—that balance had been translated into an editorial position that was quickly adopted by black publications across the country. Also thanks to the *Courier,* which was taking its cues largely from a letter from one of its readers, the position had a name as well. Called the "Double V," it urged black Americans to strive for two victories in World War II. First, there was the victory over the Axis powers, which had to be won in alliance with their white countrymen. Second, there was the victory over racial

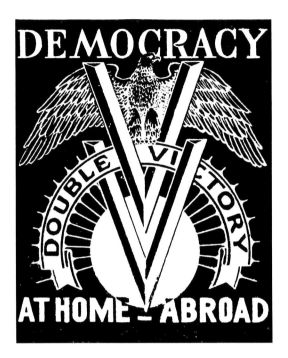

The *Pittsburgh Courier* gave birth to the "Double V" campaign by featuring this emblem on its front page, on February 7, 1942, with no explanation of what it meant. Readers nevertheless grasped its meaning immediately, and letters poured in congratulating the *Courier* on its double-barreled challenge to oppression at home as well as abroad. As this wartime theme took hold in the African American community, the "Double V" insignia began appearing on posters and sheet music, and for awhile the *Courier* appended two V's to the end of many of its war related articles. Taken from the sheet-music cover "Yankee Doodle Tan," Library of Congress, Washington, D.C.

discrimination within the United States. As the *Courier* told its readers, "In our fight for freedom we wage a two-pronged attack against our enslavers at home and those abroad who would enslave us."[2]

Commenting on the "Double V" strategy shortly after it had been articulated, one African American publication approvingly noted, "If we fight two wars . . . we can win them both. If we try to fight either alone, we can lose them both."[3] Although this analysis overlooked some other possible outcomes, it was nevertheless a wise appraisal of the situation.

But sound as it may have seemed to members of the black press, "Double V" received a decidedly cool reception elsewhere. For many members of the American white establishment, it was simply not enough that the African American press urged its readers on to such patriotic acts as enlistment in the army and the buying of war bonds while it still kept them apprised of the chronic mistreatment of blacks. By engaging in the latter, the reasoning went, it stood guilty of sowing the seeds of internal dissension at a time when the nation could ill afford it.

The most widely aired articulations of that point of view occurred in a number of commentaries by white journalists. Chief among them was a column by Westbrook Pegler, appearing in late April of 1942, which charged the African American press with demoralizing black soldiers with its incessant "race-angling of news."[4] Although Pegler did not give examples, doubtless one of the things he had in mind was the multitude of reports in the black press focusing on the many injustices—large and small—suffered by black servicemen in America's rigidly segregated armed forces. Pegler was not especially concerned that such stories were frequently all too true. All that mattered to him was their potential for sowing wartime disaffection among 10 percent of the country's population.

Pegler's and several other similar commentaries on the black press, however, were only the visible tip of a fairly deep iceberg. Many branches of the federal government were also disturbed with the black press. In the spring of 1942, for example, the Office of Facts and Figures issued one report directly linking the "Double V" campaign to an erosion of black morale, and another roundly castigating the "inflammatory extremist tenor of the Negro newspapers."[5] At the same time, the military, who saw the African American press's continual, and sometimes sensationalized, reportage of harsh mistreatment of black soldiers as a breeder of unrest within the ranks, toyed with the idea of banning black newspapers from army posts and, in fact, did so on a few occasions. For similar reasons, officials in the post office urged barring various black newspapers from being sent through the mails. Meanwhile, FBI director J. Edgar Hoover was inclined to equate the black press's unabating criticisms of America's institutionalized racism with a treasonous conspiracy. Soon he was ordering agents to, as the *Pittsburgh Courier* angrily put it, "cow [the black press] into soft-pedaling its criticism and ending its forthright exposure of the outrageous discrimination to which Negroes have been subjected."[6] Moreover, if Hoover had had his way, the measures to curb the black press would have gone yet further, and the Justice Department might well have attempted to prosecute a number of black newspapers on charges of wartime sedition.

In the end, however, the efforts to curb the African American press were only sporadic, and fell well short of that last most drastic of measures. Still, throughout much of the war, the black press was kept under government surveillance of various kinds, and more than one official continued to worry about its potential as a dangerously divisive force in the country's united struggle to subdue its Axis foes.

## GEORGE S. SCHUYLER

1895–1977

Of all the black journalists working in America during the war, perhaps none fed the anxiety among government's officialdom more than George Schuyler. A longtime staff member of the *Pittsburgh Courier*, Schuyler supplied that weekly paper with a regular column and was also one of its chief editorial writers. As such, he was in a good position to wield great influence within the black community. With a nationwide circulation of approximately two hundred and fifty thousand, the *Courier* was far and away the most widely read black newspaper in the United States; and that alone was enough to prompt the author of a wartime FBI report to conclude that "George Samuel Schuyler carries considerable weight with the Negroes . . . throughout the country."[7] But it was not just the *Courier*'s circulation figures that led to that judgment. Doubtless it also had much to do with Schuyler's journalistic style, a blend of colorful terminology, unmincing frankness, and a sometimes-withering wit, which invariably made for good reading. Writing about the African American press's response to World War II in 1943, one observer noted, "George S. Schuyler is about the best. He is a clear and vivid writer. Sometimes he writes with a mordant sarcasm, but he does not let it unbalance the order of his ideas."[8]

Simply put, Schuyler was a force to be reckoned with. Had he chosen to devote his obvious talents and position of influence exclusively to promoting support for the war among the *Courier*'s readers, he would, in all likelihood, have become the fawned-over darling of government officials concerned with wartime morale. Instead, he opted for a course that made him the object of suspicion. Shortly after Pearl Harbor, he was claiming a place of emi-

George Schuyler. Morgan Smith (1910–1993) and Marvin Smith (born 1910), not dated. Photographs and Prints Division, Schomburg Center for Research in Black Culture, The New York Public Library, Astor, Lenox and Tilden Foundations, New York City. © Morgan and Marvin Smith

## SAMPLING OF GEORGE SCHUYLER'S COMMENTARY ON WAR AND RACISM
*PITTSBURGH COURIER*, JANUARY 10, 1942

With sadness and weary resignation I note that many supposedly intelligent Negroes are swallowing hook, line and sinker the same bush-wah at which their fathers snapped during World War No. I, to wit: that once victory is achieved, the colored brethren as a reward for their patriotic efforts and sacrifices will be promptly invested with all the rights and privileges of citizenship now denied them wherever *Homo Nordicus* rules. . . .

It is not surprising that many so-called educated Negroes of the thousandaire class are avidly absorbing this brannigan. Education everywhere being an instrument of the ruling class designed to condition the mass mind to acquiescence in, acceptance of and sacrifice for the status quo, it follows that those longest and most intensively subjected to the educative process are more ready to uncritically accept the bologna offered them. . . .

On the other hand, Old Uncle Mose vegetating in Bumgut Alley is by comparison a sapient fellow. When white-collared phonographs occasionally come into his neighborhood spouting the white folks' propaganda he relieves himself of a silent and cynical chuckle. He may not be wise to the number of Negro farmers having pellegra in Shotgun, Ark., or aware of the incidence of tuberculosis among the colored denizens of the alleys of our national capital. . . . But he does know that the Crackers are not going to get off his back, voluntarily, ever.

It is this curbstone wisdom that endears me to the sable herd. Although poor, ill-housed, bulldozed by the local Gestapo, jammed into jail on the slightest pretext, rachitic, exploited, numb-brained, and unlettered, they entertain no illusions about their destiny under the Caucasian dictatorship. They believed in Santa Claus once, immediately after emancipation from chattel slavery, and suffered a grand disillusionment. They have been sceptical ever since, and nothing in their experience has tended to shake their cynicism. They know that their white folks have no intention of accepting them as brothers and sisters, friends and comrades on an equal basis, so all the bishbish about democracy, freedom and national unity leaves them as cold as a streetwalker on South Parkway.

Of course it may be that the black masses's scepticism is unwarranted and that the phonograph Negroes are correct. Maybe peace will see an end to the discrimination and insults Negroes suffer under the Stars and Stripes, Union Jack, Tri-color, the banner of Savoy, etc. I hope so. But when I see a great nation like the United States engaged in a struggle for its life and still determined to continue and even expand the racial distinctions forced upon the whole nation by the fanatically Negrophobic South, I am doubtful, to put it mildly. And unless some changes are made pretty soon in the direction of real improvement, the disinterest of the black masses in the outcome of the current fight for democracy is going to become tremendous.

nence in the forefront of black journalists who were making it their business to cast an often jarringly critical light on the United States and its war effort.

This did not mean that Schuyler thought that African Americans should not support their country in this moment of extreme crisis. In fact, he had every confidence that they would, and if they needed any prodding in that patriotic direction, he further assumed that there were plenty of other members of the black press ready and willing to undertake the task. What it did mean, however, was that Schuyler was determined that the exigencies of war should not become an excuse to "curve, duck or dodge" on matters relating to America's racial inequities, and as long as his own power of the pen held out, he would face those inequities head-on and press for their alleviation.[9] In a column published shortly after Pearl Harbor, for example, he told his readers that all the current talk "about fighting for democracy, freedom and the American Way is just so much blather as long as pigment separates an American citizen from the enjoyment of all the rights, privileges and duties of citizenship." Until now, he claimed, the United States "has yielded 100 per cent to the same racial theories trumpeted by Herr Hitler," and if the country now wanted blacks to serve loyally on both the home and military fronts, it was obliged to return the favor by stopping the practice of those theories.[10]

Unfortunately, that obligation to reciprocate went largely unrecognized in white America. Cynic that he was, this did not surprise Schuyler, and before long his writings for the *Courier* were serving as a vehicle for airing an unpleasant litany of wartime racism that included blatant, often harsh, and generally unredressed mistreatment of black enlistees in the armed services and employment discrimination against blacks in the nation's defense industries.

Among Schuyler's more effective columns regarding the wrongs suffered by black soldiers was one in which, with an irony worthy of Jonathan Swift, he suggested that all black army enlistments be trained in the South, where Negrophobia was most rampant. "Have I suddenly gone Uncle Tom?" he asked after making this proposal to place black youths in an environment where, if past experience was any gauge, they were certain to be vulnerable to virulent, and sometimes life-threatening, expressions of white racism. "No, my dearly beloved," he answered, "my crawfishing comes from Machiavellian calculation." For what better toughening process could there be for the black soldier trainee than the "baptism of fire" that he would endure in the southern setting? The more he encountered the insults, physical harassments, and humiliations at the hands of Dixie's "local Crackers," Schuyler opined, the better prepared he would be to meet the enemy in Europe and the Pacific.[11]

A good many spokesmen for the African American community were optimistic that the democratic idealism undergirding the Allied cause of World War II would ultimately bring noted improvement in the

## A CAUSE CÉLÈBRE FOR THE AFRICAN AMERICAN PRESS

### THE CASE OF DORIE MILLER

Among the basic ingredients of the African American press's "Double V" campaign of World War II were stories publicizing the heroics and distinguished service of black servicemen. In airing such stories, and on occasion giving them far bigger play than might seem warranted in retrospect, the black press had a twofold purpose in mind: One, it hoped that the stories would serve as an inspiration to the nation's black community and so strengthen its patriotic commitment to the war effort; two, it intended that these tales of courage and dedication should serve as a wedge for persuading the armed services to eliminate their barriers of racial discrimination, which so sharply limited the advancement opportunities for most black soldiers and sailors and relegated them, all too often, to noncombative menial tasks.

But publicizing black military distinctions was not always easy, and it sometimes seemed that there was a conspiracy on the part of the white establishment to prevent it. The most celebrated testimony to that possibility was the case of the black navy messman Dorie Miller (1919–1943).

"above and beyond the call of duty"

DORIE MILLER
Received the Navy Cross
at Pearl Harbor, May 27, 1942

On December 7, 1941, when Japan launched its surprise attack on the United States fleet stationed at Pearl Harbor, Miller was there serving on the battleship *Arizona,* and as Japanese planes bombed and strafed the decks of his ship, the Texas-born messman suddenly found himself thrust into a combat role for which the navy had never trained him. But, training or no training, Miller met the situation exceedingly well, and after braving enemy fire to help carry his fatally wounded commanding officer to safety, he proceeded to an unattended antiaircraft gun, which he manned until fires on the beleaguered *Arizona*'s decks forced him to abandon ship.

Later it would be claimed that Miller's marksmanship resulted in the downing of at least one Japanese plane and possibly more. The truth of that assertion is debatable. Nevertheless, one thing was certain: By the time Miller was forced to abandon ship, he had gone well beyond what the navy required of its messmen and had taken risks that clearly put him in line for some special public recognition.

Dorie Miller was precisely the kind of serviceman that the African American press wanted to extol to its readers. Unfortunately, when black newspapers first got wind of Miller's

performance at Pearl Harbor, the hero of the tale was simply described as an unidentified black messman. Worse yet, when members of the black press, led by the *Pittsburgh Courier,* asked the navy to be more specific, they encountered a wall of silence. For three months the navy flatly refused to reveal Miller's name, and only after papers like the *Courier* had repeatedly accused it of an egregiously unfair racial bias in this matter did the navy finally disclose Dorie Miller's identity and shortly thereafter bestow on him the Navy Cross.

The black press's campaign to uncover Miller's identity did considerably more than win Miller a medal and provide the African American community with its first hero of the war. It also drew decidedly unfavorable attention to the navy's practice of admitting blacks to its ranks only as lowly messmen, with no prospect whatsoever for advancement out of that category. In doing so, there was little doubt that the black press had been a major catalyst in forcing the navy in April 1942 to declare a policy permitting blacks to serve on its ships in other capacities. The change was a far cry from full racial integration, and it looked better on paper than it did in practice. Still, it was a significant start in breaking down the United States Navy's Jim Crowism.

This poster celebrating Dorie Miller's heroism was produced by the Office of War Information for distribution to black communities in the hope that awareness of Miller would solidify black support for the war effort. David Stone Martin (1913–1992), 1943. Color halftone poster, 71.1 x 51.4 cm (28 x 20¼ in.). National Portrait Gallery, Smithsonian Institution, Washington, D.C.

status of American blacks. The only major proviso was that blacks should do their part in defeating the Axis powers. Schuyler, however, was leery of that roseate hypothesis, and in a column of early 1942, he confided to his *Courier* readership that all the current "whoopdedoodle about democracy and freedom leaves me as cold as the heart of a Harlem pawnbroker."[12] As the war progressed, he saw no reason to retreat from that position. More than a year later, with the flood of examples of racial discrimination in defense industries and the armed services continuing to run strong, he ended a column on the failure of the nation's wartime leadership to stem that tide with the pessimistic declaration that "the post-war world—as I see it—will be much similar to the pre-war world if these people run it."[13]

An especially meaningful sign for Schuyler that this gloomy prognostication was correct was the sharp contrast that he noted between the self-righteous indignation expressed by American public officials at news of an Axis wartime atrocity and the passivity with which they seemed to accept atrocities committed against blacks in their own country. Schuyler produced two columns on this subject. On both occasions, he began by citing reports of the brutal mistreatment, and in some instances wanton murder, of captured white American soldiers by the Japanese and the outraged cry for vengeance that those acts had elicited from prominent government figures. Schuyler found these heated responses perfectly justifiable. But he also

saw a double standard operating. Whereas the government vowed "to spare no expense" in punishing the Japanese for their brutal excesses, he pointed out, its zeal for seeing justice done in similar domestic cases where African Americans had been the victim was decidedly less than wholehearted.[14] When, for example, a black army private on guard duty in Louisiana was shot down by a local police officer, and when a black sergeant was killed on the steps of a church in Little Rock, Arkansas, the Justice Department had on both occasions declared itself unable to prosecute the alleged assailants.

Although much of Schuyler's wartime writings for the *Courier* indicated pessimism regarding the state of the country's race relations, he was not without hope that World War II might bring some substantial gains for African Americans. To some extent, his gloomy ruminations were meant to keep his readers vigilant: whatever progress the war spawned in alleviating racial discrimination, they should not lull themselves into thinking that the battle against American racism was largely won.

Schuyler, in other words, was well aware that the country's pressing wartime labor needs had opened up good employment opportunities to blacks that they never had before. He knew as well that, his repeated harping on the barriers of discrimination in the armed services notwithstanding, some slow but measurable progress in breaking down those barriers had been made. But he also feared that the racial discrimination that had gone away due to the exigencies of war would reappear with the advent of peace.

That apprehension inspired what was one of Schuyler's most original contributions to American journalistic commentary on the war. Published in the *Crisis,* the black monthly, in late 1943, it was entitled "A Long War Will Aid the Negro," and in it Schuyler took the position that, at least as far as blacks were concerned, the longer and harder World War II was, the better would be the result. As the war taxed America's white human resources to their limit and beyond, he reasoned, the country would have to rely increasingly on blacks to meet its needs and, in the process, would open up to them yet further opportunities for advancement. Thus, whereas at the moment black military officers were strictly barred from command-

ing white soldiers, a protracted war could ultimately force a change in that policy. Similarly, the need for more and more manpower in defense industries could eventually lead to African Americans being accepted in ever more skilled and responsible jobs. In short, if the war lasted until 1949 or so, Schuyler thought, the entry of blacks into the mainstream of American life would be so far advanced that there could be no going back to the old white American habit of relegating them to the lowest rung. Doubtless such thinking, with its implied wish for a drawn-out war, would have struck a good many whites as shockingly unpatriotic and not a trifle subversive. But that was how Schuyler saw it, and true to his promise not to "curve, duck or dodge," that was how he was going to tell it.

# 9

# THE MAVERICKS

American combat correspondents of World War II generally enjoyed a generous amount of freedom in pursuing their stories at the front. That freedom, however, was by no means unbridled, and as discussed in chapter 2, there were certain fundamental rules and guidelines that they were expected to live by if they were to maintain their accreditation. Among other things, as noncombatants they were not allowed to bear arms and were prohibited from becoming active participants in such field activities as reconnaissance and intelligence gathering. Simply put, regardless of the situation they found themselves in, correspondents could not adopt the role of a combat soldier. Another ground rule demanded that correspondents abide by the censorship decisions made by the military authorities in their respective war zones, and if those authorities thought that a news story or photograph in any way jeopardized the success of a given action or the safety of soldiers, they reserved the right to amend it accordingly or even withhold it entirely. In cases, for example, where specifics about Allied troop movements or casualties seemed to offer the enemy useful insights into their opponents' strengths, weaknesses, or future strategies, a reporter's mention of them in a homebound story was promptly scratched out.

By and large, correspondents accepted such constraints on their behavior in the name of doing their part for the war effort, and although there were occasional grumblings about arbitrary censorship of a free press, the system worked pretty much to everyone's satisfaction. There were occasional attempts by journalists to circumvent the rules, but generally speaking, these end runs did not represent egregious violations. When, for example, members of the press stationed in the Pacific were banned from alerting their editors, in the midsummer of 1942, to the forthcoming attack on the Japanese at Guadalcanal in the Solomon Islands, reporter John Hersey managed to pass through an unsuspecting navy censor a cable informing his bosses at *Time* that if they were "wise men," they would know where their next cover story was coming from. This riddle-like allusion to sapience was meant to put *Time*'s New York office in mind of the biblical wise man King Solomon, and sure enough, it did. As a result, when the official word came, shortly thereafter, that the Allied invasion of the Solomons had begun, the magazine was well primed for handling it in a manner commensurate with its importance.

In several instances, however, the violations of the rules by members of the press were of a more serious nature. One such instance involved Ernest Hemingway, who, for roughly seven months in 1944, worked as a European correspondent for *Collier's;* another involved Edward Kennedy of the Associated Press.

## ERNEST HEMINGWAY
1899-1961

When *Collier's* snagged Ernest Heming-way in the spring of 1944 to serve as a feature reporter in the European theater of operations, the magazine had accomplished a coup that its editors doubtless reveled in. As author of such critically acclaimed novels and short stories as *The Sun Also Rises,* "The Snows of Kilimanjaro," and *For Whom the Bell Tolls,* he was by now a literary lion of the first rank. What was more, his stint as a reporter for the North American Newspaper Alliance during the Spanish Civil War had established his reputation as a capable combat journalist.

Hemingway, too, was more than a little pleased with his new correspondent's role. Obsessively preoccupied, both in his writings and personal life, with physical courage under perilous circumstances, he relished war as the ultimate proving ground for manly bravery and endurance. The trouble with this interest in combat, however, was that Hemingway was not content with simply observing and chronicling the art of soldiering. He was too much the man of action for that, and it was almost inevitable that his impulses to participate in the war would collide with the prohibition, by international agreement, against correspondents' direct involvement in military action.

Among the first signs of that inevitability was Hemingway's article "Voyage to

War correspondent Ernest Hemingway. Unidentified photographer, 1944(?). John F. Kennedy Library, Boston. © Pan American Airways

Victory," published in *Collier's* on July 22, 1944. The first offering to appear in the magazine from its "famed war correspondent," the piece was a report of what he had seen from a troop landing craft off the northern French coast on the first day of the Normandy invasion.[1] Hemingway had been pretty much only a sideline observer on that historic occasion and, in fact, had not even been allowed to wade onto the beaches with the rest of his craft's human cargo. Instead, once the boat had accomplished its mission, its pilot, after picking up some wounded soldiers from earlier invasion waves, had returned Hemingway to a transport that promptly took the writer safe and sound to an English port. Clearly Hemingway had wanted to be at the heart of the invasion. As if to compensate for his disappointingly peripheral involvement, "Voyage to Victory," with its generous use of "I" and "we," created a distinct impression that the completion of the mission of the landing craft Hemingway was on had hinged largely on the writer's sage advice and direction to the pilot.

But first-person-singular suggestiveness on the written page was not enough to satisfy Hemingway's yearning for active participation. By August 19, he was with American troops about twenty-five miles southwest of Paris, and during the final Allied drive to retake the French capital from the Germans, Hemingway at last became an unofficial soldier in the war. Meeting up with a band of French Resistance fighters at the town of Rambouillet, he was soon using his considerable influence with American army officers to procure arms for them, and his hotel room, with its piles of grenades and machine guns, took on the aspect of a full-fledged military arsenal. Meanwhile, he was also leading his new French friends on reconnaissance missions to pinpoint remaining pockets of German resistance between Rambouillet and Paris.

Affectionately known among his companions from the Resistance as "le grand capitaine" and "colonel," Hemingway was happier than he had been in years. His current activities, he later boasted, were "straight out of Mosby," and his adrenaline was running at full tide.[2] But although all this playing at guns and drums sent Hemingway's adrenaline surging, his martial behavior was giving some of his fellow correspondents in the Rambouillet area a severe case of rising bile. As they saw it, Hemingway's activities represented a scandalous violation of wartime press rules, and it was not long before a protest to that effect was making its way to American army authorities.

The army recognized that this communication contained serious charges that had to be investigated and that, if the charges proved to be true, Hemingway would have to be disaccredited. The problem was that Hemingway had many officer friends who had enthusiastically abetted his reconnaissance operations and who thought, moreover, that he had rendered invaluable service in facilitating the Allied drive toward Paris. That, combined with the fact that the writer's great celebrity was

John Groth, the artist who did this drawing of Hemingway at Germany's Siegfried Line in September 1944, spent a good deal of time with him in the American front lines. Having done so, he concluded that Hemingway much preferred being in combat to writing about it. "He lived and breathed war. He seemed like one of the heroes in his books of war," Groth later wrote. And, when his editor's deadlines periodically compelled him to leave the fighting for awhile to churn out an article, "he looked unhappy." John Groth (1908–1988), 1944. Ink and wash on paper, 76.2 x 101.6 cm (30 x 40 in.). Art Collection, Harry Ransom Humanities Research Center, the University of Texas at Austin

This document, authorizing Hemingway to secure weapons from an army ordnance unit, goes some way in corroborating the charge that his hotel room at Rambouillet became a veritable arsenal of small arms. It also is a testament to the spell that Hemingway's macho charm cast over so many military officers and that led to their willingness to abet his appetite for battlefront adventurism. Ernest Hemingway Papers, John F. Kennedy Library, Boston

bound to inspire considerable publicity in the event of his disaccreditation, was enough to make the army officials fearful that coming down hard on Hemingway would make them look foolishly punctilious.

Consequently, although Hemingway was ordered to appear at a formal hearing to answer the charges against him, the officer charged with examining him was not interested in probing any too deeply into the actual facts of his behavior. When Hemingway blandly explained away the Resistance fighters' habit of addressing him as captain as an amiable courtesy with no meaning behind it, his interrogator accepted the reply. And when the writer disingenuously claimed that he had accompanied the Resistance sorties around Rambouillet strictly in the interest of gathering material for a story, his questioner accepted it at face value. So it was that Hemingway beat "the rap," as he put it, and the journalist-turned-warrior left the hearing with firm assurances that he was completely exonerated.

Pro forma as these proceedings were, most individuals subjected to them would likely have come away with second thoughts about repeating the offense that had brought them there in the first place. Not Hemingway. Convinced that he was above the rules governing most mortals, and enjoying the role of soldier far too much to give it up, he was, by mid-November 1944, joining American combat forces in Germany's Hurtgen Forest with a Thompson submachine gun casu-

ally and openly slung over his shoulder. A week later, he was in the thick of it once again, helping to repulse an attack of German soldiers on American lines and to knock out a German mortar.

After the war, Hemingway remained bitter that he had been forced to officially deny his central role in the reconnaissance operations around Rambouillet. A number of high officers whom he had known and assisted there also thought that an injustice had been done. To make amends, one of them, General Raymond Barton, sent through a recommendation asking that Hemingway be awarded the army's Bronze Star. Deliberately sidestepping certain details that would have clearly demonstrated Hemingway's blatant violation of a fundamental rule of war, the recommendation was approved. On June 13, 1947, he received the Bronze Star with a citation lauding him for "meritorious service" as a war correspondent.[3]

## EDWARD KENNEDY

1905-1963

Like most members of the press covering the war in areas that came under military authority, Associated Press reporter Edward Kennedy accepted military censorship as a fact of his professional life and recognized its legitimacy as an important tool in preventing potentially useful information from reaching the enemy. To be sure, as AP's bureau chief in Europe, and as a seasoned journalist who had been covering the war in Europe since 1939 and had endured its many frontline hazards as much as any reporter, he had seen more than a few cases where overzealous army censors had exceeded the guidelines of their mandate for monitoring the news. Then, too, like a good many reporters, he seems to have engaged, from time to time, in circumventing the censors and violating other regulations set down by the army's press authorities in Europe. In the file kept on him by the army, there were, for example, notations speculating that occasionally he may have crossed the borders to neutral Spain and Switzerland to file stories that he knew would be heavily altered, or suppressed altogether, by the army censors at the front, where he was currently working. Yet another memo in his file claimed that in 1944 he had ventured up to American lines in France from the Italian theater of war without gaining proper authorization from the army's press officers to do so. But although Kennedy

Edward Kennedy at Anzio beachhead in Italy, early 1944. Sam Goldstein (life-dates unknown). AP/Wide World Photos

Pictured here is the Third Reich's Colonel General Alfried Jodl signing the German surrender on May 7, 1945, at Reims. Flanking him are his aide Major Wilhelm Oxenius (*left*) and German Admiral Hans Georg von Friedeburg (*right*). United States Army Signal Corps photographer, not dated. Still Picture Branch, National Archives, Washington, D.C.

was no goody-two-shoes, he was by and large a rule-abiding correspondent and was generally as willing as anyone to play along with the army press office's censors.

There came a point, however, where Kennedy had had quite enough of World War II's censorship. It was early May 1945. With Allied armies in firm control of large chunks of Germany itself, with Hitler dead from suicide, and with the German will to fight all but gone, it was well understood that total German surrender to the Allies was in the offing. The only questions left unanswered were when, where, and how it would take place.

On Sunday, May 6, Kennedy became one of the first members of America's European press corps, based in Paris, to learn the particulars regarding those three most basic queries of his profession. Informed by army press officers that a plane was now preparing to carry seventeen reporters to the Supreme Headquarters Allied Expeditionary Force (SHAEF) at the French town of Reims to witness an event "the nature of which could not be disclosed," he did not have to be a genius to figure out what the event was.[4] So, when told that there was a seat on that plane for an AP correspondent, he had no hesitation in deciding that he would be AP's representative on this occasion.

By early evening, Kennedy and the sixteen other privileged reporters were being ushered into a red-brick technical school at Reims. At 2:41 A.M. on May 7, he was standing in a classroom, pad and pencil in hand, as two tired German generals, soberly seated across from representatives of their Allied opposition, fixed their signatures to an agreement formally and unconditionally ending the six-year conflict in Europe. Kennedy was privy to one of the most momentous, and undoubtedly the happiest, stories to come out of the war so far. As he landed back in Paris with the other correspondents a few hours later, just as a sunny dawn broke over the French capital, the professional satisfaction of this press veteran who had witnessed the beginnings of the war in Europe back in 1939 was understandably substantial.

There was, however, one fly in the ointment. Under pressure from the Soviet Union, which wanted a second surrender-signing under its auspices in Berlin, where its armies were in control, the order had come to SHAEF from Washington, D.C., that release of stories on the Reims surrender for publication would have to be delayed until the Berlin ritual was completed and the three heads of the Allied powers—Churchill, Truman, and Stalin—had personally announced the surrender to their respective peoples. Naturally, Kennedy was chagrined at this directive, as were all the other correspondents who had been at Reims. At the same time, since

hostilities had ceased and therefore no issue of military security was involved, he was doubtful that the delay order was a valid exercise of the army's censorship prerogatives. Even so, he was willing enough to sit on the story during his first hours back in Paris.

Kennedy's spirit of cooperative forbearance soon began to dissipate when he heard that French General François Savez, who had been at the surrender, had already sent his personal account of the event to the Paris newspaper *Figaro*. It diminished further yet when word reached him from London that loudspeakers were being set up at 10 Downing Street for use by Prime Minister Churchill, and that all civilian and military personnel at the nearby British war ministry had been apprised of the surrender. In other words, it was clear that in at least one Allied capital, the cat was all but out of the bag, and it was beginning to look as if the advantage of covering the surrender firsthand was soon going to turn into no advantage at all. But the leakage did not end there. A little after 2:00 P.M., Kennedy heard a radio broadcast, originating from a sector in Germany under Allied control, informing the German people that the war was formally over. He could only presume—and, as it turned out, correctly—that the broadcast was being made with an Allied blessing, which meant, of course, that SHAEF was violating its own demand for secrecy.

The normally cool and self-restraining Kennedy could stand it no more. Confronting army press officer Colonel Rob-

Floyd Davis's picture of the bar in the Hotel Scribe depicts this major Paris watering hole for war correspondents as a center of relaxed camaraderie and goodwill. At noon on May 9, 1945, however, the bar's customary bonhomie turned sour as fifty-four of Kennedy's professional peers gathered there to denounce his scoop on the German surrender and pronounce him guilty of the "most disgraceful . . . double-cross in the history of journalism." Floyd Davis (1896–1966), 1944. Oil on canvas, 48.3 x 73.7 cm (19 x 29 in.). National Portrait Gallery, Smithsonian Institution, Washington, D.C.

Key to numbered diagram of the picture
 1. Floyd Davis, *Life* field artist
 2. Gladys Rockmore Davis, *Life* field artist
 3. David Scherman, *Life* photographer
 4. Janet Flanner, *New Yorker* correspondent
 5. William Shirer, CBS newscaster
 6. Ernest Hemingway, *Collier's* correspondent
 7. A. J. Liebling, *New Yorker* correspondent
 8. Merrill Mueller, NBC correspondent
 9. H. V. Kaltenborn, NBC correspondent
10. Richard de Rochemont, *March of Time* producer
11. Bill Reusswig, King Features illustrator
12. Ham Green, *American Legion Magazine* correspondent
13. Bob Cromie, *Chicago Tribune* correspondent
14. Hugh Schuck, *New York Daily News* correspondent
15. Will Lang, *Time* correspondent
16. Lee Miller, *Vogue* photographer
17. Graham Miller, *New York Daily News* correspondent
18. Donald MacKenzie, *New York Daily News* correspondent
19. Robin Duff
21. Ralph Morse, *Life* photographer
26. Charles Wertenbaker, *Time-Life* correspondent
28. Robert Capa, *Life* photographer
29. Noel Busch, *Life* correspondent
20, 22–25, 27. Unidentified

ert Merrick in Merrick's office, he informed the officer of what was happening, and when the colonel still insisted that the correspondents from Reims could not send out their own surrender stories, Kennedy replied that he was going to send his anyway. Confident that Kennedy could not get his story out of Paris, because all outgoing lines were supposedly carefully monitored by the army, Merrick responded that he could just go ahead and try.

Kennedy, however, knew that he could make good on his defiant declaration. A few days earlier, he had discovered a telephone line to London that was not being

New Yorkers jamming Wall Street to celebrate the German surrender a day prematurely, at least as far as Allied military authorities in Europe were concerned. Unidentified photographer, not dated. UPI/Bettmann

monitored, and shortly after leaving Merrick's office, he was seated at a telephone reading his surrender dispatch while an AP staffer in London transcribed it at the other end. By 9:00 A.M., United States eastern standard time, on May 7, his story had reached New York. By afternoon, while jubilant crowds milled through the streets of every American city, newspapers across the country were carrying his account of the surrender, and by the next day, when SHAEF had planned on allowing the Reims correspondents to release their stories, the final chapter in the Allied victory in Europe was old news.

Clearly Kennedy's determination and resourcefulness had earned him a scoop of the first magnitude. But it had come at great cost. With the discovery that he had preempted them, his fellow correspondents in Paris were outraged. At a meeting of reporters convened at the city's Hotel Scribe, a letter to SHAEF, ultimately signed by fifty-four attendees, was drawn up, accusing Kennedy of "the most disgraceful, deliberate and unethical double cross in the history of journalism," and demanding that he be promptly disaccredited by the army and that AP in general be barred from operating in Europe.[5] The army was also angered, and although its blanket ban of AP lasted only a short time, Kennedy was indeed permanently shorn of his war correspondent's credentials.

Meanwhile, back in the United States, Kennedy's behavior was unleashing a

heated debate in the nation's newspapers. Some papers, most notably the prestigious *New York Times,* declared that Kennedy's violation of army censorship was unforgivable. But others—and by Kennedy's later tabulation the vast majority—thought that, given the premature leak of the surrender story, his action was well justified, especially since no threat to military security was involved. However gratifying this support may have been for Kennedy, it did not save him from becoming a pariah within his own news organization. On arriving home, he soon found that AP, though not unfriendly and unsympathetic to his cause, was finding him to be an embarrassment. Accordingly, in the fall of 1945, his connection with it was quietly cut when Kennedy, with no written or oral notification, found a large amount of money credited to his checking account. The unexpected windfall was his severance pay.

An immensely personable and capable man, Kennedy was by no means broken by this turn of events, and he went on after the war to become a much-esteemed newspaper editor in Santa Barbara and Monterey, California. Moreover, he never doubted for a minute that what he had done on May 7, 1945, had been the right course of action. In retrospect, most would agree. Today, there is a plaque in a California park dedicated to his memory, which, recalling his final act as a war correspondent, reads: "He gave the world 24 hours more of happiness."[6]

Daniel De Luce (*center*) with members of the Greek army engaged in fighting off the German-Italian invasion of their homeland. Unidentified photographer, 1941. Courtesy Daniel De Luce

## DE LUCE ON DA LOOSE

"De Luce is on da loose." By the summer of 1943, that phrase had become an often repeated pun around the offices of Associated Press. It referred to AP reporter Daniel De Luce (born 1911) and was testament to the ability of this lanky, blue-eyed journalist to get around in the current global conflict. The compliment was well deserved. Stationed in Eastern Europe in 1939, he had watched German forces massing themselves in August in Czechoslovakia for the invasion of Poland and was among the first to report that turn of events. The following month he was seated in a hotel room in Poland itself, trying to get out dispatches on the fall of that country amid the unnerving reverberations of massive German bombing raids. After witnessing Italy's conquest of Albania and the fall of Greece to the Axis, he went on to the Middle East to observe British-Soviet operations in Iran, and by the spring of 1942 he was in Burma covering the ignominious collapse of Allied resistance to a Japanese invasion. The next year found him with Anglo-American forces as they fought their way through North Africa and Sicily and finally onto the Italian mainland.

But the ultimate demonstration of De Luce's enterprising mobility came in the fall of 1943. At the moment he was assigned to British forces bogged down on Italy's eastern coast, and finding the news potential wanting in that particular corner of the war, he decided it was time to look for his stories in another venue. His choice was Yugoslavia, news of which in the Allied press had at best been spotty and impressionistic ever since the Germans had occupied it in the spring of 1941. Although it was known that a Partisan guerrilla army was actively engaged in efforts to weaken the German hold over Yugoslavia, particulars about the strength, effectiveness, and organization of this movement remained unknown. And it was those particulars that De Luce now wanted to find out about.

But wanting and getting were two different things, and when De Luce applied to British army authorities for permission to cross the Adriatic into Yugoslavia, he was quickly told that it would be impossible. Due largely to the strong communist orientation of much of its membership, the Yugoslav Partisans posed political difficulties for the Allies, and the last thing that was wanted, it seemed, was an independent newsman filing stories calling attention to those difficulties. De Luce, however, remained undeterred. In late September, having

De Luce's Greek press credentials. Courtesy Daniel De Luce

secretly arranged to cross the Adriatic in a small wooden craft, he landed on Yugoslavia's Dalmatian coast, where in rainy predawn darkness he crept into a wood to make contact with two Partisans who had been told through a trans-Adriatic grapevine to expect him. Shortly thereafter, De Luce was being welcomed into a Partisan headquarters high in the Dinaric Alps, where he began absorbing the nuts-and-bolts details of the Allies' most mysterious and least-known armies.

De Luce stayed with the Partisans only a few days, but by the time he got back to Italy, he had completed a series of five stories that undeniably constituted a major scoop. Not surprisingly, the British authorities did not share in De Luce's sense of triumph, and although they let most of his stories pass through censorship largely as they had been written, they squashed one of the pieces altogether, because it probed too deeply into the postwar implications of the Partisans' strongly communist leadership. They also toyed with taking disciplinary measures against De Luce but in the end contented themselves with simply redoubling their determination to prevent future efforts at news coverage of the Yugoslav Partisans. But while his venture into forbidden territory ruffled military feathers, it impressed America's Fourth Estate, and the following spring his series made him the recipient of a Pulitzer Prize.

# 10

# DAWN OF THE ATOMIC AGE

## WILLIAM LAURENCE AND JOHN HERSEY

The test explosion of the first atomic bomb, pictured here, melted the sand of the New Mexico desert into a "glasslike substance," Laurence later noted, and the flash of light generated by it could be seen 450 miles away. Shock waves from the detonation caused windows to rattle in buildings as far away from ground zero as 235 miles. Unidentified photographer, 1945. Los Alamos National Laboratory, New Mexico

In a debate about the single most significant news story of World War II, some might argue that it was Hitler's marching into Poland or Great Britain's survival of the German air blitzes over its cities. Others might say that it was the invasion of Normandy or the Japanese attack on Pearl Harbor or the Allied triumph at Guadalcanal. Moreover, the justifications for these, as well as several other choices, would doubtless appear sound and reasonable. But it would also be fair to say that there was one story from the war that seems to loom above all others—the detonation of the atomic bombs over Hiroshima and Nagasaki, Japan, in August 1945. Not only did the unleashing of this most devastating of military weapons finally force the Japanese to surrender and so end the most destructive conflict in history. More important, it also altered forever the way human civilization looked at its wars and its technological progress. For, as news spread of the atomic bomb's use and its enormous power, the realization quickly sank into humanity's collective consciousness that it was now armed with the means to willfully destroy itself in an astonishingly quick fashion.

Hundreds of reporters covered the story of the atomic bomb at the time of its unveiling. But two stand out from the rest. One was William Laurence, whose lucid coverage of the development of this weapon and its ultimate use was largely responsible for introducing Americans to its technical complexities and the potentials of atomic energy for both constructive and destructive purposes. The other was John Hersey, who, following the Japanese surrender, examined the effect of the atomic bomb at Hiroshima in terms of its human victims.

## WILLIAM LAURENCE
1888–1977

William Laurence, nicknamed after his affiliation with the Manhattan Project "Atomic Bill." Unidentified photographer for the *New York Times,* 1955. The New York Times Company Archives, New York City

For William Laurence, the potential for, if not the actuality of, the weapon that completely decimated Hiroshima on August 6, 1945, with a single earth-shattering blast was somewhat of an old story. A Pulitzer Prize–winning science reporter for the *New York Times,* the Lithuanian-born Lau-

rence, whose youthful flirtation with political radicalism had forced him in 1905 to flee his native land secreted in a barrel, brought two exceptional talents to his journalistic specialty. One, he possessed an unfailing ability to translate the complexities of modern science into terms comprehensible to the average layman. Two, he had an uncanny gift for spotting the practical implications of arcane scientific discoveries, sometimes even before the scientists themselves did. As a result, when he began hearing, in the late 1930s, about the success of several physicists in splitting the atoms of a difficult-to-isolate type of uranium known as uranium-235, he was quick to grasp the mind-boggling possibilities of that development for both good and ill. He was also quick to reduce those possibilities into easily understandable terms. By the summer of 1940, first in the *New York Times* and then in the *Saturday Evening Post,* he was publishing lengthy articles informing the general American public on how the fission of atoms, in surprisingly small quantities of U-235, could propel an ocean liner indefinitely, heat and light entire cities, or set off a destructive bomb blast that was the equivalent of twenty thousand tons of TNT.

To a large degree, Laurence looked positively on the advent of these not fully developed potentials. Granted, the physics community had not yet figured out how to efficiently isolate sufficient quantities of U-235 to make it a viable source of energy, and furthermore, it would probably

be a good number of years before it did. Nevertheless, when the riddle of that important detail was finally solved, he opined, it was bound to transform modern civilization largely for the better.

Still, there was one aspect of atomic fission that, especially in light of the present world situation, greatly troubled Laurence. With Hitler currently overrunning Europe and no signs that his zest for conquest was abating, what would happen should German scientists succeed in developing an atomic weapon before anyone else did? The answer to that nagging question was obvious: It was perfectly conceivable that the countries of the world, the United States included, would become pawns totally at the Third Reich's mercy. What was more, as Laurence well knew, there were German physicists who were as conversant with the present knowledge on nuclear fission as their counterparts elsewhere, and even as he wrote his articles on that phenomenon in 1940, they might be well launched on a Nazi-sponsored drive to develop an atomic bomb.

Laurence thus hoped that his pieces for the *Times* and the *Saturday Evening Post* would serve as an alarm that might compel a concentrated effort to develop nuclear fission's potential before somebody else did. As he put it many years later, his message to both the United States government and the scientific community was that, regardless of the cost, "Here is something that we can't afford not to do."[1] At first, he was not at all confident that his articles had convinced anyone, when the only

noteworthy response in the United States Congress was a speech by a California congressman demanding that atomic power not be investigated any further, lest it ruin the oil and coal industries and lead to massive unemployment.

But gradually there were other indications pointing to the strong likelihood that, if not his articles, then something else was hastening this country's investigations into the atomic mysteries of U-235. For starters, Laurence found that physicists who had always been more than willing to chat with him about this or that phase of their trade were avoiding him at meetings and not answering his telephone calls. Then, after Pearl Harbor and America's entry as a full participant in World War II, he began to notice that some well-known scientists of his acquaintance were disappearing from sight altogether. Equally significant, in mid-1942 he himself received a letter from the United States Office of Censorship asking him not to write on certain subjects, including U-235, and to refrain from printing any speculations about possible German progress in the field of nuclear fission. From these bits and pieces, Laurence soon became reasonably certain that an American effort to develop an atomic weapon before the Germans did was under way. Finally, when a recently drafted college student to whom he had periodically offered vocational advice came to him one day and announced that the army was assigning him to its "most secret ... plant in the country," whatever lingering concern he may have

Despite the remoteness of the site in New Mexico chosen for testing the first atomic bomb, Manhattan Project administrators worried that the explosion would be noticed hundreds of miles away and would therefore invite questions from the local press. Thus, among Laurence's first tasks for the project was drafting a post-testing news release meant to satisfy this curiosity. This is one of his three drafts—each tailored to meet varying degrees of noticeability—explaining that a large ammunition magazine had accidentally blown up at Alamogordo Air Base. Following the actual bomb test, that was indeed the story given out; to the Manhattan Project's relief, the press accepted it, no questions asked. Military Reference Branch, National Archives, Washington, D.C.

had that the United States was not earnestly engaged in such a venture quickly evaporated.[2]

For a long while, however, it appeared to Laurence that, beyond knowing the existence of a top-secret atomic project and not being at liberty to report even that, thanks to wartime censorship, he was not going to be privy to this latter-day Promethean story until well after it had run its full course. But what this ace science reporter did not know was just how deeply his 1940 articles on atomic power had impressed some of their more important readers. In fact, there was enough government concern that his discourses on the atom might somehow help the enemy that the FBI requested the nation's public li-

braries to report anyone showing an interest in Laurence's *Saturday Evening Post* article. More to the point, by the early months of 1945, the government's high regard for Laurence's ability to write lucidly about atom splitting was taking a more positive turn as far as Laurence's own professional fortunes were concerned. The army-sponsored Manhattan District Project, charged with developing an atomic bomb, had by then advanced far enough to suggest that it might well have a usable weapon in the final effort to subdue the Axis powers. That being the case, the project felt a need for a trustworthy spokesman, capable of understanding atomic energy's complexities and, once the weapon was unveiled, of providing the public with

clear accounts of what it was all about. That individual was William Laurence, and in the mid-spring of 1945, he was talking to Manhattan Project head General Leslie Groves about taking leave from the *New York Times* to become the inside chronicler of the greatest weapons story of the war.

In undertaking this assignment, Laurence could not tell even his wife what he was doing or where he was doing it. Neither could he rush to a phone, as was his reporter's instinct, whenever he saw a new

phase of the Manhattan Project, to dictate an article on it for the *Times*. Nevertheless, there were ample compensations for such drawbacks. For a man such as Laurence, whose scientific curiosity was insatiable, being granted nearly absolute freedom to question and observe at the Manhattan Project's various top-secret sites across the country inspired comparisons to the proverbial child let loose in a candy store. Laurence relished every minute of this ground-floor experience and attacked with gusto the challenge of explaining the ad-

Manhattan Project staff work on installing the world's first atomic bomb in a steel tower in preparation for its detonation near Alamogordo, New Mexico, in July 1945. Bill Laurence later recalled that this task engendered considerable anxiety. One scientist was so unnerved that he finally had to be removed from the site. Unidentified photographer. Los Alamos National Laboratory, New Mexico

vent of the Atomic Age to an as-yet-unsuspecting public.

So, through May, June, and early July of 1945, Laurence was busy visiting the various sites of the Manhattan Project, scattered from Tennessee to Washington State. Initially, even for his retentive mind, "it was very difficult to absorb it all."[3] But he grew adjusted to the daily flood of highly complex scientific data, and he was soon converting his notes into articles on the many phases of atomic energy, which were to be released to the press whenever it was deemed appropriate to make the atomic bomb public knowledge. Meanwhile, as the articles were completed, his notes were systematically destroyed, and the articles themselves were all stored in a well-secured safe. Also stowed in the safe was a speech Laurence drafted for President Truman against the day when he would be called upon to officially announce the atomic bomb's wartime use.

Laurence's experience as the Manhattan Project's inside reporter had two climaxes. The first occurred the morning of July 16, when he witnessed the first test explosion of an atomic bomb in the desert near Alamogordo, New Mexico. At this point, the necessity of stifling his reporter's instinct to tell his editors what he had seen became hardest to bear. Here he was, an eyewitness to something that he later likened to "the moment of creation," and unable to tell the world about it.[4]

Then, some three weeks later, came the second climax—the first, second, and only uses of an atomic weapon in the history of war. On August 6, Laurence was on an island in the Pacific watching the plane *Enola Gay* as it cautiously lifted off the runway, loaded with the most powerful bomb ever conceived, and set its course toward Hiroshima, Japan. Two days later, Laurence himself was on a plane loaded with a similar weapon and headed toward the Japanese town of Nagasaki, where he was to observe firsthand the wartime use of atomic energy.

By then, Laurence's venture into undercover news reporting had come to its intended fruition. With his stories about the bomb now released to the press, they were being aired in newspapers across the country, and Americans were absorbing, over their morning coffee, the enormous implications of what they said. Unfortunately for Laurence, however, these stories had not been distributed in a way that clearly assigned their authorship. As a result, Laurence's exclusive scoop became public domain. In his own *New York Times,* for example, the first story about the atomic bomb on the day following its drop on Hiroshima appeared beneath another reporter's byline. Nevertheless, Laurence ultimately got his due. Returning to the *Times* shortly after the Nagasaki mission, he began writing his own series of articles about the discovery of atomic fission and the development of the atomic bomb, for which he eventually received his second Pulitzer Prize.

## JOHN HERSEY
1914–1993

By the time John Hersey arrived in Japan, in January 1946, to write a story for the *New Yorker* on the effect of the atomic bomb on the inhabitants of Hiroshima, his stature as a chronicler of World War II was well established. In fact, had he chosen not to undertake this final piece on the conflict, his place in the ranks of the war's most talented reporters would nevertheless have been quite secure. As a correspondent for *Time* and *Life* who had covered the war in both the Pacific and in Europe, he had manifested gifts for wartime journalism that seemed on occasion to be unique.

From his experience at the battle for Guadalcanal in the fall of 1942, for example, he had drawn a story about a failed Marine sortie along the island's Matanikau River that, when translated into a small

This picture of John Hersey was taken in late 1945 in China, just before he went to Hiroshima to begin gathering his story of the atomic bomb. Hersey was aboard a boat on the Yangtze River and, in collaboration with photographer Dmitri Kessel, was doing a never-published picture story for *Life* on the life of that great Asian waterway. Dmitri Kessel (born 1902) for *Life* magazine. Courtesy estate of John Hersey

volume called *Into the Valley,* evoked the discomforts and fears of Pacific jungle fighting as few wartime accounts did, and led one critic to proclaim its author as "a new Hemingway."[5] Also among the fruits of his war correspondent's work was a best-selling novel, *Bell for Adano,* which won a Pulitzer Prize and became the basis for a Broadway play. Modeled on identifiable events and people Hersey had observed during the invasion of Sicily in the summer of 1943, the book focused on the difficulty the Allies faced in reestablishing civil order as their armies liberated Italy, and although *Adano* was fiction, many critics considered it imperative reading for anyone seeking to understand that particular problem. Adding yet further to Hersey's distinction was a pair of articles for *Life,* where he artfully melded conventions of fictional storytelling with hard reporting to chronicle the severe problems facing many American soldiers on their return to civilian status as a result of both physical and psychological wounds.

But substantial though Hersey's reporting accomplishments were, and well-seasoned though he may have been in translating the traumatic chaos of war into readable prose, Hersey initially felt a bit daunted when he confronted the prospect of doing a three-part article on Hiroshima for the *New Yorker.* As he later put it, "The problem of how to deal with such a massive event was very, very . . . difficult to figure out."[6] One possible, and perhaps the most obvious, solution that crossed his mind, as he headed toward Japan late in

1945, was a panoramic one, where the jumping-off point would be such things as statistics relating to the physical destruction of buildings and the thousands upon thousands of people killed and irremediably maimed by the bomb. Ultimately, however, Hersey rejected that alternative after an officer of the ship he was traveling on brought him the ship's library copy of Thornton Wilder's 1927 novel, *The Bridge of San Luis Rey.* A tale about the collapse, in 1714, of a bridge spanning a deep gorge in Peru, the book centered on the lives of the five people whom fortune had tragically placed on the bridge at the moment of its destruction. Confined to sick bay with a touch of the flu when he began reading this five-stranded narrative, Hersey was not far into it before he knew that he had found the organizing strategy for his story on Hiroshima: Taking his cue from Wilder, he would tell it through the lives of some of the city's inhabitants who had survived the atomic bomb.

Hersey naturally knew that the number of people he could treat to good effect in his story in its final form would be fairly limited. But when he reached the "huge flat expanse of waste" that Hiroshima been reduced to in the wake of the atomic bomb, his reporter's instinct for thoroughness compelled him, initially at least, to cast his net widely.[7] With the help of Jesuit missionaries, he began interviewing some twenty-five or thirty survivors. Then, as the interviewing process progressed, his number of subjects gradually declined. By the time he felt himself ready to begin writing his account, he was focusing on the experiences of six people who had been at Hiroshima on August 6, 1945—two doctors, a German Catholic priest, a Japanese Protestant minister, a widowed seamstress, and a young factory office girl.

Behind this final selection lay no sociologist's concern for achieving a representative cross section of Hiroshima's population. Nor was the choice necessarily dictated by the fact that these individuals had endured the most dramatic or tragic experiences as a result of the atomic bomb. Rather, Hersey settled on these six people as the vehicle for telling his story chiefly because they had been some of his most forthcoming interview subjects. Ultimately that criterion proved to be sound enough. As Hersey began weaving their respective accounts of the bombing and its aftermath into a single continuous narrative, he was creating one of the most lasting pieces of journalistic literature to come out of World War II.

The strength of Hersey's *Hiroshima* rests mainly in an assiduously observed self-restraint that generally kept its author from editorially intruding into his subjects' narrative and indulging in histrionic asides about the atomic bomb's cataclysmic nature. When Hersey finally submitted his manuscript to the *New Yorker,* the editors recognized that virtue and the overall unity that it gave to the work. As a result, it was quickly realized that some of the work's impact would be lost if the magazine carried out its original intention

to serialize it, and so they decided to devote one entire issue to it instead.

For a publication that was known and loved for its urbanity and sophisticated banter, this represented a drastic departure from the norm. But the decision proved to be a wise one. When the *New Yorker*'s August 31, 1946, issue appeared on the newsstands with Hersey's sobering chronicle of the human cost of the atomic bomb, it sold out almost immediately, and figures such as Albert Einstein were requesting reprints. That, however, was only the beginning. Soon three English newspapers were asking for the right to publish *Hiroshima* in the British Isles; ABC was reading it in its entirety over the radio; the Book of the Month Club was distributing it in book form as a premium to its membership; and

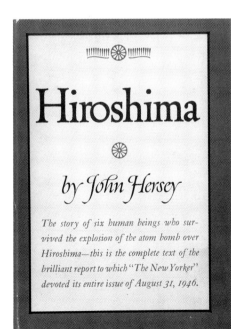

Since this Book-of-the-Month-Club edition appeared in 1946, *Hiroshima* has never been out of print. Courtesy estate of John Hersey

View of Hiroshima, near "point zero," shortly after the dropping of the atomic bomb. Still Picture Branch, National Archives, Washington, D.C.

by fall it was being translated into half-a-dozen foreign languages.

Within a week of its appearance, Hersey's report on Hiroshima had generated a response that ranked it as the most-talked-about journalistic accomplishment in the annals of World War II, and perhaps in the whole history of the Fourth Estate. Just why it did is not difficult to fathom. Many other reporters had already chronicled the mind-boggling power of the atomic bomb and its effects on the 240,000 inhabitants of Hiroshima in considerable detail. But as one critic pointed out, they "had bellowed at us and exhorted us, and thundered. They numbed us with statistics of infinity and the hieroglyphics of formulae we could not understand."[8] Hersey, on the other hand, had shown the good judgment to relate this year-old news story in a manner that sought to explain its meanings for mankind in the eminently comprehensible terms of some of its victims. Even after nearly fifty years, this piece has not lost its immediacy. As its six protagonists move through their respective experiences—from the initial bomb blast and their first reactions, once they realized that they had survived it, to their later bouts with radiation sickness—they still impart a sense of the event that is almost palpable.

# NOTES

## 1. IN ON THE GROUND FLOOR

1. *Time,* September 4, 1939, p. 34.

2. *Newsweek,* September 18, 1939, p. 36.

3. Julia Edwards, *Women of the World: The Great Foreign Correspondents* (Boston: Houghton Mifflin, 1988), p. 59.

4. Photocopy of Colonel Robert McCormick to J. L. Maloney, May 26, 1939, Sigrid Schultz Papers (Mass Communications History Center, State Historical Society of Wisconsin, Madison).

5. Edwards, *Women of the World,* p. 59.

6. *Time,* August 28, 1939, p. 20.

7. Leland Stowe, *Nazi Germany Means War* (London: Faber & Faber, 1933), pp. 67–68.

8. Leland Stowe, *No Other Road to Freedom* (New York: Alfred A. Knopf, 1941), p. 153.

9. Robert St. John, *This Was My World* (Garden City, N.Y.: Doubleday, 1953), p. 367.

10. *New York Times,* January 17, 1942.

## 2. THE NATION'S SECURITY VS. THE RIGHT TO KNOW

1. Byron Price, memoirs, Byron Price Papers (Mass Communications History Center, State Historical Society of Wisconsin), pp. 209, 224.

2. Ibid., p. 299.

3. Ibid., p. 293.

4. Ibid., p. 352.

5. W. S. Gilmore to Byron Price, August 23, 1945; Sayre (Pennsylvania) *Evening Times,* August 24, 1945, Byron Price Papers.

6. Theodore F. Koop, *Weapon of Silence* (Chicago: University of Chicago Press, 1946), p. 270.

7. Eric Larrabee, *Commander in Chief: Franklin Delano Roosevelt, His Lieutenants, and Their War* (New York: Harper & Row, 1987), p. 155.

8. Thomas B. Buell, *Master of Sea Power* (Boston: Little, Brown, 1980), p. 149.

9. Joseph A. Bors, Hamilton [illegible], Sandor S. Klein to Admiral Ernest J. King, October 1, 1943, Admiral Ernest King Papers, Library of Congress.

10. Elmer Davis to Admiral Ernest J. King, March 2, 1943, Admiral Ernest King Papers, Library of Congress.

11. Buell, *Master of Sea Power*, p. 252.

12. Lewis Sebring, "The MacArthur Circus," manuscript, Lewis Sebring Papers (Mass Communications History Center, State Historical Society of Wisconsin, Madison), p. 19.

13. Ibid., p. 20.

14. Ibid., p. 94.

15. D. Clayton James, *The Years of MacArthur*, vol. 2 (Boston: Houghton Mifflin, 1975), p. 602.

16. Sebring, "The MacArthur Circus," p. 57.

17. *Time*, June 22, 1942, p. 21.

18. Cedric Larson, "OWI's Domestic News Bureau: An Account and Appraisal," *Journalism Quarterly* 26 (March 1949): 3.

19. Elmer Davis, "Report to the President," ed. Ronald T. Farrar, *Journalism Monographs* 7 (August 1968): 42.

20. Cedric Larson, "OWI's Domestic News Bureau," p. 13.

21. Joseph Gies, *The Colonel of Chicago* (New York: E. P. Dutton, 1979), p. 205.

## 3. PUTTING THE WAR IN FOCUS

1. Jonathan Silverman, *For the World to See: The Life of Margaret Bourke-White* (New York: Viking Press, 1983), p. 102.

2. Vicki Goldberg, *Margaret Bourke-White: A Biography* (New York: Harper & Row Publishers, 1986), p. 245.

3. Ibid., p. 247.

4. Richard Whelan, *Robert Capa: A Biography* (New York: Alfred A. Knopf, 1985), p. 143.

5. Ibid., p. 151.

6. Ibid., p. 211.

7. Ibid., p. 187.

8. Ibid., p. 212.

9. Robert Capa, *Images of War* (New York: Grossman Publishers, 1964), p. 109.

10. "Beachheads of Normandy," *Life*, June 19, 1944, p. 26.

11. Whelan, *Capa*, p. 238.

12. Carl Mydans, *More Than Meets the Eye* (New York: Harper & Brothers, 1959), p. 68.

13. Ibid., p. 63.

14. Carl Mydans, "My God! It's Carl Mydans," *Life*, February 19, 1945, p. 93.

15. Antony Penrose, *The Lives of Lee Miller* (New York: Holt, Rinehart and Winston, 1985), p. 139.

16. Lee Miller, "Germans Are Like This," *Vogue*, June 1945, p. 105.

17. Jim Hughes, *W. Eugene Smith: Shadow & Substance* (New York: McGraw-Hill, 1989), p. 133.

18. W. Eugene Smith, *His Photographs and Notes* (New York: Aperture, 1969), p. 20.

19. Hughes, *W. Eugene Smith*, p. 143.

20. Ibid., p. 170.

21. Joe Rosenthal, with W. C. Heinz, "The Picture That Will Live Forever," *Collier's* 135 (February 18, 1955): 62.

22. Ibid., p. 64.

## 4. NO JOB FOR A WOMAN

1. Lilya Wagner, *Women War Correspondents of World War II* (Westport, Conn.: Greenwood Press, 1989), p. 7.

2. Ibid., p. 11.

3. Wilda M. Smith and Eleanor A. Bogart, *The Wars of Peggy Hull: The Life and Times of a War Correspondent* (El Paso: Texas Western Press, 1991), p. 71.

4. Ibid., p. 94.

5. *Cleveland Plain Dealer*, February 29, 1944.

6. Smith and Bogart, *Wars of Peggy Hull*, p. 244.

7. Transcript of interview with Helen Kirkpatrick by Anne S. Kasper, Women in Journalism Oral History Project of the Washington Press Club Foundation, April 3–5, 1990, p. 13.

8. Wagner, *Women War Correspondents*, p. 75.

9. Julia Edwards, *Women of the World: The Great Foreign Correspondents* (Boston: Houghton Mifflin, 1988), p. 110.

10. Interview with Helen Kirkpatrick, pp. 61–62.

## 5. THE WORM'S EYE VIEW OF THE WAR

1. Frederick Painton, "The Hoosier Letter-Writer," *More Post Biographies*, ed. John E. Drewry (Athens: University of Georgia Press, 1946), p. 280.

2. Ernie Pyle, *Ernie's War: The Best of Ernie Pyle's World War II Dispatches*, ed. David Nichols (New York: Random House, 1986), pp. 8–9.

3. Ibid., p. 10.

4. Lee G. Miller, *The Story of Ernie Pyle* (New York: Viking Press, 1950), pp. 246, 262–63.

5. Pyle, *Ernie's War*, p. 10.

6. "Ernie Pyle," *Life*, November 15, 1943.

7. Miller, *Ernie Pyle*, p. 279.

8. Painton, "Hoosier Letter-Writer," p. 288.

9. Lincoln Barnett, "Ernie Pyle," *Life*, April 2, 1945, p. 105.

10. Pyle, *Ernie's War*, pp. 23–24.

11. Paul Lancaster, "Ernie Pyle: Chronicler of 'The Men Who Do the Dying,'" *American Heritage* 32 (February/March 1981): 38.

12. Ibid., p. 40.

13. Miller, *Ernie Pyle*, p. 428.

14. Bill Mauldin, *The Brass Ring* (New York: W. W. Norton, 1971), pp. 200, 201.

15. Mrs. Andrew Carter to Bill Maul-

din, June 29, 1945, papers in the possession of Bill Mauldin.

16. Mauldin, *Brass Ring,* p. 199.

17. Ibid., p. 261.

18. Ibid., p. 264.

19. *Time,* March 26, 1945, p. 60.

20. Harry C. Butcher, *My Three Years with Eisenhower* (New York: Simon and Schuster, 1946), p. 796.

21. Taped interview with Bill Mauldin at his home in Santa Fe, New Mexico, December 10, 1992 (National Portrait Gallery, Smithsonian Institution).

## 6. BROADCASTING THE WAR

1. *Newsweek,* September 11, 1939, p. 42.

2. *Newsweek,* June 19, 1944, p. 95.

3. Edward R. Murrow, *In Search of Light: The Broadcasts of Edward R. Murrow, 1938–1961,* ed. Edward Bliss, Jr. (New York: Alfred A. Knopf, 1967), p. 4.

4. Joseph E. Persico, *Edward R. Murrow: An American Original* (New York: McGraw-Hill, 1988), p. 144.

5. Ibid., p. 238.

6. Murrow, *In Search of Light,* p. 78.

7. William L. Shirer, *Berlin Diary: The Journal of a Foreign Correspondent, 1934–1941* (New York: Alfred A. Knopf, 1941), p. 501.

8. Ibid., p. 333.

9. Ibid., p. 511.

10. *Time,* June 23, 1941, p. 92.

## 7. ARTISTS AS FIELD CORRESPONDENTS

1. *Washington Star,* June 18, 1943.

2. *Washington Star,* June 20, 1943.

3. George Biddle, *Artist at War* (New York: Viking Press, 1944), p. 55.

4. Ibid., pp. 123–24.

5. George Biddle, *George Biddle's War Drawings* (New York: Hyperion Press, 1944), p. 2.

6. Biddle, *Artist at War,* p. 202.

7. Ibid., p. 172.

8. Rafael Steinberg, *Island Fighting* (Alexandria, Va.: Time-Life Books, 1978), p. 174.

9. Tom Lea, *Battle Stations: A Grizzly from the Coral Sea Peleliu Landing* (Dallas, Tex.: Still Point Press, 1988), p. 75.

10. Tom Lea, *A Picture Gallery* (Boston: Little, Brown, 1968), p. 94.

11. Undated draft of letter from David Fredenthal to Edith Halpert, circa 1935, David Fredenthal Papers (Archives of American Art, Washington, D.C.)

12. *Life,* September 11, 1944, p. 11.

13. *Art Digest* 19 (February 15, 1945): 12.

14. Aaron Bohrod, *A Decade of Still Life* (Madison: University of Wisconsin Press, 1966), p. 25.

15. Transcript of Aaron Bohrod war diary, Forbes Watson Papers (Archives of American Art, Washington, D.C.), p. 13.

16. Ibid., p. 37.

17. Ibid., p. 46.

18. *Time,* July 19, 1943, p. 47.

## 8. THE AFRICAN AMERICAN PRESS IN WARTIME

1. Martin Blumenson, *Patton: The Man Behind the Legend, 1885–1945* (New York: William Morrow, 1985), p. 210.

2. *Pittsburgh Courier,* February 14, 1942.

3. Lee Finkle, *Forum for Protest* (Cranbury, N.J.: Associated University Presses, 1975), p. 118.

4. *New York World Telegram,* April 28, 1942.

5. Patrick S. Washburn, *A Question of Sedition* (New York: Oxford University Press, 1986), p. 108.

6. Quoted in ibid., p. 84.

7. Edward Welsh, "Was George Schuyler Pro-Japanese?" paper (Ohio University, 1986), p. 2.

8. Thomas Sancton, "The Negro Press," *The New Republic* 108 (April 26, 1943): 559.

9. *Pittsburgh Courier,* January 3, 1943.

10. Ibid.

11. Ibid., February 28, 1942.

12. Ibid., April 11, 1942.

13. Ibid., May 22, 1943.

14. Ibid., May 8, 1943, and February 12, 1944.

## 9. THE MAVERICKS

1. Ernest Hemingway, "Voyage to Victory," *Collier's* 114 (July 22, 1944): 11.

2. Carlos H. Baker, *Ernest Hemingway: A Life Story* (New York: Charles Scribner's Sons, 1969), p. 411.

3. Ibid., p. 461.

4. Edward Kennedy, "I'd Do It Again," *Atlantic Monthly* 182 (August 1948): 37.

5. *New York Times,* May 9, 1945.

6. Gordon Cubbison, "An Extra Day of Happiness," *The Herald Weekend Magazine* of the *Monterey Peninsula Herald,* May 4, 1975, p. 4.

## 10. THE DAWN OF THE ATOMIC AGE

1. Transcript of interview with William L. Laurence, Oral History Research Office, Columbia University (1964), p. 275.

2. Ibid., p. 281.

3. Ibid., p. 295.

4. Ibid., p. 318.

5. *Time,* March 15, 1943, p. 9.

6. Transcript of videotape interview with John Hersey, September 29, 1991 (National Portrait Gallery, Smithsonian Institution), p. 15.

7. Ibid., p. 16.

8. Charles Poore, "'The Most Spectacular Explosion in the Time of Man,'" *New York Times Book Review,* November 10, 1946, p. 7.

# SELECTED BIBLIOGRAPHY

Bainbridge, John. "Significant Sig and the Funnies." *New Yorker* 19 (January 9, 1944): 25–35.

Baker, Carlos H. *Ernest Hemingway: A Life Story.* New York: Charles Scribner's Sons, 1969.

Belford, Barbara. *Brilliant Bylines: A Biographical Anthology of Notable Newspaperwomen in America.* New York: Columbia University Press, 1986.

Biddle, George. *Artist at War.* New York: Viking Press, 1944.

———. *George Biddle's War Drawings.* New York: Hyperion Press, 1944.

Bohrod, Aaron. Wartime memoir. Forbes Watson Papers, Archives of American Art, Smithsonian Institution.

Bourke-White, Margaret. *Portrait of Myself.* New York: Simon and Schuster, 1963.

Brown, David, and W. Richard Bruner, eds. *How I Got That Story.* New York: E. P. Dutton, 1967.

Buell, Thomas B. *Master of Sea Power: A Biography of Fleet Admiral Ernest J. King.* Boston: Little, Brown, 1980.

Burlingame, Roger. *Don't Let Them Scare You: The Life and Times of Elmer Davis.* New York: J. B. Lippincott, 1961.

Capa, Robert. *Slightly Out of Focus.* New York: Henry Holt, 1945.

Culbert, David Holbrook. *News for Everyman: Radio and Foreign Affairs in Thirties America.* Westport, Conn.: Greenwood Press, 1976.

Davis, Elmer. *The Office of War Information, 13 June 1942–15 September 1945: Report to the President.* Austin, Tex.: Journalism Monographs, no. 7 (August 1968).

Edwards, Julia. *Women of the World: The Great Foreign Correspondents.* Boston: Houghton Mifflin, 1988.

Emery, Edwin, and Henry Ladd Smith. *The Press in America.* New York: Prentice-Hall, 1954.

Finkle, Lee. *Forum for Protest.* Cranbury, N.J.: Associated University Presses, 1975.

Gies, Joseph. *The Colonel of Chicago.* New York: E. P. Dutton, 1979.

Goldberg, Vicki. *Margaret Bourke-White: A Biography.* New York: Harper & Row, 1986.

Hersey, John. *Into the Valley.* New York: Alfred A. Knopf, 1943.

———. *Hiroshima.* New York: Alfred A. Knopf, 1946.

Hohenberg, John. *Foreign Correspondence: The Great Reporters and Their Times.* New York: Columbia University Press, 1964.

Hughes, Jim. *W. Eugene Smith: Shadow and Substance.* New York: McGraw-Hill, 1989.

James, D. Clayton. *The Years of MacArthur.* Boston: Houghton Mifflin, 1975.

Kennedy, Edward. "I'd Do It Again." *Atlantic Monthly* 182 (August 1948): 36–41.

Knightley, Phillip. *The First Casualty.* New York: Harcourt Brace Jovanovich, 1975.

Koop, Theodore F. *Weapon of Silence.* Chicago: University of Chicago Press, 1946.

Lacayo, Richard, and George Russell. *Eyewitness: 150 Years of Photojournalism.* New York: Oxmoor House, 1990.

Laurence, William L. *Dawn over Zero: The Story of the Atomic Bomb.* New York: Alfred A. Knopf, 1946.

———. "The Reminiscences of William L. Laurence." Oral History Research Office, Columbia University, 1964.

Layton, Rear Admiral Edwin T., with Captain Roger Pineau and John Costello. *"And I Was There": Pearl Harbor and Midway – Breaking the Secrets.* New York: William Morrow, 1985.

Lea, Tom. *A Picture Gallery.* Boston: Little, Brown, 1968.

———. *Battle Stations: A Grizzly from the Coral Sea Peleliu Landing.* Dallas, Tex.: Still Point Press, 1988.

Livingston, Jane. *Lee Miller Photographer.*

New York: Thames and Hudson, 1989.

Marling, Karal Ann, and John Whetenhall. *Iwo Jima: Monuments, Memories, and the American Hero.* Cambridge, Mass.: Harvard University Press, 1991.

Mathews, Joseph J. *Reporting the Wars.* Minneapolis: University of Minnesota Press, 1957.

Mauldin, Bill. *Up Front.* Cleveland: World Publishing, 1945.

———. *The Brass Ring.* New York: W. W. Norton, 1971.

Meyers, Jeffrey. *Hemingway: A Biography.* New York: Harper & Row, 1985.

Milbank, Helen Kirkpatrick. Interview with Anne S. Kasper, April 1990. Women in Journalism Oral History Project of the Washington Press Club.

Miller, Lee G. *The Story of Ernie Pyle.* New York: Viking Press, 1950.

Moeller, Susan D. *Shooting War: Photography and the American Experience of Combat.* New York: Basic Books, 1989.

Morris, Joe Alex. *Deadline Every Minute: The Story of the United Press.* Garden City, N.Y.: Doubleday, 1957.

Mydans, Carl. *More Than Meets the Eye.* New York: Harper & Brothers, 1959.

———. *Carl Mydans, Photojournalist.* New York: Harry N. Abrams, 1985.

Oestreicher, John C. *The World Is Their Beat.* New York: Duell, Sloan and Pearce, 1945.

Oldfield, Barney. *Never a Shot in Anger.* New York: Duell, Sloan and Pearce, 1956.

Penrose, Antony. *The Lives of Lee Miller.* New York: Holt, Rinehart and Winston, 1985.

Perlin, Bernard. "Liberation Will Find the Greeks Are Ready." *Life,* September 4, 1944.

———. Taped interview with Frederick Voss, October 1992. National Portrait Gallery, Smithsonian Institution.

Persico, Joseph E. *Edward R. Murrow: An American Original.* New York: McGraw-Hill, 1988.

Pratt, Fletcher. "How the Censors Rigged the News." *Harper's Magazine* 192 (February 1946): 97–105.

Price, Byron. Memoir. Byron Price Papers, State Historical Society of Wisconsin, Madison.

Pyle, Ernie. *The Best of Ernie Pyle's World War II Dispatches.* Edited with a biographical essay by David Nichols. New York: Random House, 1986.

Rosenthal, Joe. Transcript of interview with Benis M. Frank, June 25, 1975. Oral History Division, United States Marine Corps Museum.

Rosenthal, Joe, with W. C. Heinz. "The Picture That Will Live Forever." *Collier's* 135 (February 18, 1955): 62–67.

St. John, Robert. *From the Land of the Silent People.* Garden City, N.Y.: Doubleday, Dorand, 1942.

———. *This Was My World.* Garden City, N.Y.: Doubleday, 1953.

———. *Foreign Correspondent.* Garden City, N.Y.: Doubleday, 1957.

Sanders, David. *John Hersey.* New York: Twayne Publishers, 1967.

Schultz, Sigrid. Transcript of interview with Harold Hutchings for *Chicago Tribune* Archives, April 5–6, 1977. Sigrid Schultz Papers, State Historical Society of Wisconsin, Madison.

Sebring, Lewis. "The MacArthur Circus" (manuscript). Lewis Sebring Papers, State Historical Society of Wisconsin, Madison.

Shirer, William L. *Berlin Diary: The Journal of a Foreign Correspondent, 1934–1941.* New York: Alfred A. Knopf, 1941.

———. *20th Century Journey: The Nightmare Years, 1930–1940.* Boston: Little, Brown, 1984.

Smith, W. Eugene. *W. Eugene Smith: Master of the Photographic Essay.* Edited with commentary by William S. Johnson. New York: Aperture, 1981.

Smith, Wilda M., and Eleanor A. Bogart. *The Wars of Peggy Hull: The Life and Times of a War Correspondent.* El Paso: Texas Western Press, 1991.

Sperber, A. M. *Murrow: His Life and Times.* New York: Freundlich, 1986.

Stein, Meyer L. *Under Fire: The Story of American War Correspondents.* New York: Julian Messner, 1968.

Stowe, Leland. *Nazi Germany Means War.* London: Faber & Faber, 1933.

———. *No Other Road to Freedom.* New York: Alfred A. Knopf, 1941.

———. Transcript of interview with John D. Stewart, March 22–23, 1982. Leland Stowe Papers, State Historical Society of Wisconsin, Madison.

Thomas, Byron. Wartime memoir. Byron Thomas Papers. Archives of American Art, Smithsonian Institution.

Tregaskis, Richard. *Guadalcanal Diary.* New York: Random House, 1943.

———. *Invasion Diary.* New York: Random House, 1944.

Wagner, Lilya. *Women War Correspondents of World War II.* Westport, Conn.: Greenwood Press, 1989.

Washburn, Patrick S. *A Question of Sedition: The Federal Government's Investigation of the Black Press During World War II.* New York: Oxford University Press, 1986.

Whelan, Richard. *Robert Capa: A Biography.* New York: Alfred A. Knopf, 1985.

# INDEX

*Italicized page numbers refer to illustrations.*

This book was acquired for Smithsonian Institution Press by Mark Hirsch. The manuscript was edited by Frances Stevenson and Dru Dowdy of the National Portrait Gallery and by Jack Kirshbaum of Smithsonian Institution Press. The book's production was managed by Ken Sabol, and it was designed by Linda McKnight. The text was composed on an Agfa Selectset 5000 by Graphic Composition, Inc., of Athens, Georgia. The text typeface is Times Roman, which was commissioned by *The Times* of London in 1931 and designed by Stanley Morison. The display face is Franklin Gothic Ultra Condensed, designed by Morris Benton in 1912. The book was printed on 80-lb. Lustro Offset Enamel paper by D. W. Friesen and Sons of Altoona, Manitoba, Canada.